Fish of Illinois

FIELD GUIDE

by Dave Bosanko

Adventure Publications, Inc.
Cambridge, MN

ACKNOWLEDGEMENTS

Special thanks to the U.S. Fish and Wildlife Service, and the Illinois and Minnesota Departments of Natural Resources.

Edited by Brett Ortler

Cover and book design by Jonathan Norberg

Illustration credits by artist and page number:
Cover illustrations: Brook Trout (main) and Bluegill (upper and back cover) by Duane Raver/USFWS

Timothy Knepp/USFWS: 110 (main), 112, 124, 126 **MyFWC.com/fishing** 11 **Duane Raver/USFWS:** 10 (bottom), 19, 24, 26, 28, 30, 32, 34, 36, 38, 44, 46, 48, 50, 52, 56, 58, 68, 72, 94, 106, 114, 116 (main), 120, 142, 144, 146, 158, 160, 164, 166, 168, 170, 174, 176, 178, 182, 186, 188 **Joseph Tomelleri** 10 (top), 40 (both), 42, 54, 60, 62, 64, 66, 70, 74, 76 (both), 78, 80, 82, 84 (both), 86 (both), 88, 90, 92, 96, 98, 100, 102, 104, 108, 110 (inset), 116 (inset), 118 (both), 122, 128, 130, 132, 134, 136, 138, 140, 148, 150, 152, 154, 156, 162, 172, 180, 184, 190, 192

10 9 8 7 6 5 4 3 2 1

Copyright 2009 by David Bosanko
Published by Adventure Publications, Inc.
820 Cleveland St. S
Cambridge, MN 55008
1-800-678-7006
www.adventurepublications.net
Printed in China
ISBN-13: 978-1-59193-219-2
ISBN-10: 1-59193-219-X

TABLE OF CONTENTS

How To Use This Book 8
Fish Anatomy 10
Fish Names 13
About Illinois Fish 13
Frequently Asked Questions 14
Fish Diseases 16
Invasive Species 17
Fun With Fish 17
Catch-And-Release Fishing 18
Fish Measurement 19
Illinois Master Angler State Records 20
Fish Consumption Advisories 21
Example Page 22

Bowfin Family——————————————————————
    Bowfin .... bowfin group 24

Catfish Family—————————————————————
    Black Bullhead .... bullhead group 26
    Brown Bullhead .... bullhead group 28
    Yellow Bullhead .... bullhead group 30
    Blue Catfish .... catfish group 32
    Channel Catfish .... catfish group 34
    Flathead Catfish .... catfish group 36
    White Catfish .... catfish group 38
    Stonecat .... madtom group 40
    Tadpole Madtom .... madtom group 40

Cod Family———————————————————————————
    Burbot .... freshwater cod group 42

Drum Family
Freshwater Drum .... freshwater drum group 44

Eel Family
American Eel................. freshwater eel group 46

Gar Family
Longnose Gar.................gar group 48
Shortnose Gar ....gar group 50
Spotted Gar ....gar group 52

Goby Family
Round Goby...................goby group 54

Herring Family
Alewife................herring group 56
Skipjack Herring ....herring group 58
Gizzard Shad.................shad group 60
Threadfin Shad..............shad group 62

Lamprey Family
Native Lampreys ...... freshwater lamprey group 64
Sea Lamprey .... marine lamprey group 66

Livebearer Family
Mosquitofish................gambusia group 68

Minnow Family
Bighead Carp................carp group 70
Common Carp.................carp group 72
Grass Carp ....carp group 74
Goldfish ....carp group 76
Silver Carp ....carp group 78

4

Creek Chub...................................... chub group 80
Southern Redbelly Dace................dace group 82
Fathead Minnow .... minnow group 84
Golden Shiner .... shiner group 86

Mooneye Family
Goldeye ....mooneye group 88
Mooneye ....mooneye group 90

Mudminnow Family
Central Mudminnow .... mudminnow group 92

Paddlefish Family
Paddlefish .... paddlefish group 94

Perch Family
Johnny Darter........................ darter group 96
Sauger.......................... pike-perch group 98
Saugeye ....pike-perch group 100
Walleye ....pike-perch group 102
Logperch......................... logperch group 104
Yellow Perch..................yellow perch group 106

Pike Family
Grass Pickerel...................... pike group 108
Muskellunge/Tiger Muskie.......pike group 110
Northern Pike .... pike group 112

Salmon Family
Brook Trout .... char and trout group 114
Brown Trout............. char and trout group 116
Lake Trout................ char and trout group 118

5

Rainbow Trout............ char and trout group 120
Chinook Salmon.............salmon group 122
Coho Salmon..................salmon group 124
Pink Salmon ....salmon group 126
Cisco ....whitefish group 128

Sculpin Family--
Mottled Sculpin ...... freshwater sculpin group 130

Silverside Family--
Brook Silverside .....freshwater silverside group 132

Smelt Family--
Rainbow Smelt .... landlocked smelt group 134

Stickleback Family--
Brook Stickleback .... stickleback group 136

Sturgeon Family--
Lake Sturgeon ....freshwater sturgeon group 138
Shovelnose Sturgeon. freshwater sturgeon group 140

Sucker Family--
Bigmouth Buffalo ....buffalo group 142
Black Buffalo....................buffalo group 144
Smallmouth Buffalo ....buffalo group 146
Quillback .... carpsucker group 148
Shorthead Redhorse .... redhorse group 150
Silver Redhorse................ redhorse group 152
Northern Hog Sucker........... sucker group 154
White Sucker..................... sucker group 156

Sunfish Family

Largemouth Bass............. black bass group 158

Smallmouth Bass............ black bass group 160

Spotted Bass .... black bass group 162

Black Crappie ....crappie group 164

White Crappie ....crappie group 166

Bluegill...................true sunfish group 168

Green Sunfish .... true sunfish group 170

Longear Sunfish .... true sunfish group 172

Orangespotted Sunfish.... true sunfish group 174

Pumpkinseed .... true sunfish group 176

Redear Sunfish .... true sunfish group 178

Rock Bass................. true sunfish group 180

Warmouth................. true sunfish group 182

Temperate Bass/Striped Bass Family

Hybrid Striped Bass..... freshwater bass group 184

White Bass .... freshwater bass group 186

Striped Bass............... marine bass group 188

Yellow Bass .... freshwater bass group 190

Topminnow Family

Blackstripe Topminnow....topminnow group 192

Glossary 194

Primary References 199

Index 200

About the Author 208

HOW TO USE THIS BOOK

Your *Fish of Illinois Field Guide* is designed to make it easy to identify more than 80 species of the most common and important fish in Illinois and learn fascinating facts about each species' range, natural history and more.

The fish are organized by families, such as Catfish (*Ictaluridae*), Perch (*Percidae*), Trout and Salmon (*Salmonidae*) and Sunfish (*Centrarchidae*), which are listed in alphabetical order. Within these families, individual species are arranged alphabetically in their appropriate groups. For example, members of the Sunfish family are divided into Black Bass, Crappie and True Sunfish groups. For a detailed list of fish families and individual species, turn to the Table of Contents (pp. 3-7); the Index (pp. 200-207) provides a reference guide to fish by common name (such as Lake Trout) and other common terms for the species.

Fish Identification

Determining a fish's body shape is the first step to identifying it. Each fish family usually exhibits one or sometimes two basic outlines. Catfish have long, stout bodies with flattened heads, barbels or "whiskers" around the mouth, a relatively tall but narrow dorsal fin and an adipose fin. There are two forms of Sunfish: the flat, round, plate-like outline we see in Bluegills, and the torpedo or "fusiform" shape of Largemouth Bass.

In this field guide you can quickly identify a fish by first matching its general body shape to one of the fish family silhouettes listed in the Table of Contents (pp. 3-7). From there, turn to that family's section and use the illustrations and text descriptions to identify your fish. Sample Pages (pp. 22-23) are provided to explain how the information is presented in each two-page spread.

For some species, the illustration will be enough to identify your catch, but it is important to note that your fish may not look exactly like the artwork. Fish frequently change colors. Males that are brightly colored during the spawning season may show muted coloration at other times. Likewise, bass caught in muddy streams show much less pattern than those taken from clear lakes—and all fish lose some of their markings and color when removed from the water.

Most fish are similar in appearance to one or more other species—often, but not always, within the same family. For example, the Black Crappie is remarkably similar to the White Crappie. To accurately identify such look-alikes, check the inset illustrations and accompanying notes below the main illustration, under the "Similar Species" heading.

Throughout *Fish of Illinois* we use basic biological and fisheries management terms that refer to physical characteristics or conditions of fish and their environment, such as dorsal fin or turbid water. For your convenience, these are listed and defined in the Glossary (pp. 194-198), along with other handy fish-related terms and their definitions.

Understanding such terminology will help you make sense of reports on state and federal research, fish population surveys, lake assessments, management plans and other important fisheries documents.

FISH ANATOMY

To identify fish, you will need to know a few basic terms that apply to fins and their locations.

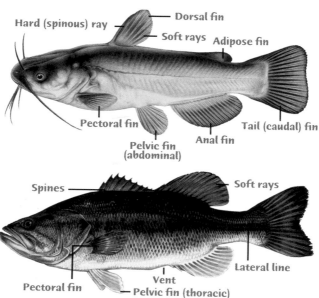

Fins are made up of bony structures that support a membrane. There are three kinds of bony structures in fins. **Soft rays** are flexible fin supports that are sometimes branched. **Spines** are stiff, often sharp supports that are not jointed. **Hard rays** are stiff, pointed, barbed structures that can be raised or lowered. Catfish are famous for their hard rays which are mistakenly called spines. Sunfish have soft rays associated with spines to form a dorsal fin.

Fins are named by their position on the fish. The **dorsal fin** is on the top along the midline. A few fish have another fin on their back called an **adipose fin**. This is a small, fleshy protuberance located between the dorsal fin and the tail and is distinctive of trout and catfish.

On each side of the fish near the gills are the **pectoral fins**. The **anal fin** is located along the midline on the fish's bottom or ventral side. There is also a paired set of fins on the bottom of the fish called the **pelvic fins**. Pelvic fins can be in the **thoracic position** just below the pectoral fins or farther back on the stomach in the **abdominal position**. The tail is known as the **caudal fin**.

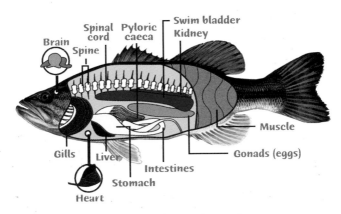

Eyes—A fish's eyes can detect color. Their eyes are rounder than those of mammals because of the refractive index of water; focus is achieved by moving the lens in and out, not by distorting light as mammals do. Different species have varying levels of eyesight. Walleyes can see well in low light, while Bluegills have excellent daytime vision but see poorly at night. Catfish have bad eyes night or day.

Nostrils—A pair of nostrils, or *nares*, is used to detect odors in the water. Eels and catfishes have particularly well-developed senses of smell.

Mouth—The shape of the mouth is a clue to what the fish eats. The larger the food it consumes, the larger the mouth.

Teeth—Not all fish have teeth, but those that do have teeth designed to help them feed. Walleyes, northern pike and muskies have sharp *canine* teeth for grabbing and holding prey. Minnows have *pharyngeal* teeth—located in the throat—for grinding. Catfish have *cardiform* teeth, which feel like a rough patch in the front of the mouth. Bass have tiny patches of *vomerine* teeth in the roof of their mouths.

Swim Bladder—Almost all fish have a swim bladder, a balloon-like organ that helps the fish regulate its buoyancy.

Lateral Line—This sensory organ helps the fish detect movement in the water (to help avoid predators or capture prey) as well as water currents and pressure changes. It consists of fluid-filled sacs with hair-like sensors, which are open to the water through a row of pores in their skin along each side—creating a visible line along the fish's side.

FISH NAMES

A Walleye is a Walleye in Illinois. But in the northern parts of its range, Canadians call it a jack or jackfish. In some areas it is often called a pickerel or walleyed pike.

Because common names may vary regionally, and even change for different sizes of the same species, scientific names are used that are exactly the same around the world. Each species has only one correct scientific name that can be recognized anywhere, in any language. The Walleye is *Sander vitreus* from Chicago to Copenhagen.

Scientific names are made up of Greek or Latin words that often describe the species. There are two parts to a scientific name: the generic or "genus," which is capitalized (*Sander*), and the specific name, which is not capitalized (*vitreus*). Both are displayed in italic text.

A species' genus represents a group of closely related fish. The Walleye and Sauger are in the same genus, so they share the generic name *Sander*. But each have different specific names, *vitreus* for Walleye, *canadensis* for the Sauger.

ABOUT ILLINOIS FISH

Illinois is a large agricultural state with much of the landscape devoted to grain production. Home to large cities and an ever-expanding industrial complex, Illinois also supports a variety of aquatic habitats. Large rivers like the Mississippi, the Ohio, and the Illinois border and divide the state. Illinois is also home to midsized rivers like the Big Muddy, the Kaskaskia and the Wabash, not to mention countless small streams and creeks. There are glacial lakes in the northeast, gigantic Lake Michigan to the north and large reservoirs and small farm ponds are present throughout the state.

In the extreme southern portion of the state, there are even cypress-tupelo swamps reminiscent of the Deep South.

This variety of aquatic habitat has led to a great diversity of fish species. In all, there are over 200 fish species that now reside in Illinois. Some of these fish are threatened or endangered due to drastic environmental changes such as increased agricultural and industrial runoff and habitat destruction. Introduced species, including those introduced accidentally and intentionally, are also part of the picture.

Only a fraction of Illinois' fish are represented in this book. The 30 or so species targeted by recreational fishermen are included, as are another 50 species that are of particular interest to those who spend time near the water, either because these species are baitfish or they have some unique or interesting characteristic.

FREQUENTLY ASKED QUESTIONS

What is a fish?

Fish are aquatic, typically cold-blooded animals that have backbones, gills and fins.

Are all fish cold-blooded?

All freshwater fish are cold-blooded. Recently it has been discovered that some members of the saltwater Tuna family are warm-blooded. Whales and Bottlenose Dolphins are also warm-blooded, but they are mammals, not fish.

Do all fish have scales?

No. Most fish have scales that look like those on the Common Goldfish. A few, such as Alligator Gar, have scales that resemble armor plates. Catfish have no scales at all.

How do fish breathe?

A fish takes in water through its mouth and forces it through its gills, where a system of fine membranes absorbs oxygen from the water and releases carbon dioxide. Gills cannot pump air efficiently over these membranes, which quickly dry out and stick together. Fish should never be out of the water longer than you can hold your breath.

Can fish breathe air?

Some species can; gars have a modified swim bladder that acts like a lung. Fish that can't breathe air may die when dissolved oxygen in the water falls below critical levels.

How do fish swim?

Fish swim by contracting bands of muscles on alternate sides of their body so the tail is whipped rapidly from side to side. Pectoral and pelvic fins are used mainly for stability when a fish hovers, but are sometimes used during rapid bursts of forward motion.

Do all fish look like fish?

Most do and are easily recognizable as fish. The eels and lampreys are fish, but they look like snakes. Sculpins look like little goblins with bat wings.

Where can you find fish?

Some fish species can be found in almost any body of water, but not all fish are found everywhere. Each species has adapted to exploit a particular habitat. A species may move around within its home water, sometimes migrating hundreds of miles between lakes, rivers and tributary streams. Some movements, such as spawning migrations, are seasonal and very predictable.

Fish may also move horizontally from one area to another, or vertically in the water column, in response to changes in environmental conditions and food availability. In addition, many fish have daily travel patterns. By studying a species' habitat, food and spawning information in this book—and understanding how it interacts with other Illinois fish—it is possible to make an educated prediction of where to find it in any lake, stream or river.

FISH DISEASES

Fish are susceptible to various parasites, infections and diseases. One of the newest threats is viral hemorrhagic septicemia (VHS) virus, a serious pathogen of fresh and saltwater fish that is causing an emerging disease in the Great Lakes region of the United States and Canada. VHS virus affects fish of all sizes and age ranges. It does not pose a threat to human health, but VHS has been blamed for fish kills in lakes Huron, St. Clair, Erie, Ontario, Conesus and Skaneateles, and the St. Lawrence River. The VHS virus has recently been found in some Wisconsin lakes and Lake Michigan.

In June 2007, fish health regulations were finalized to prevent the spread of viral hemorrhagic septicemia (VHS) and other fish diseases into Illinois. For more information visit the Illinois Department of Natural Resources website at www.dnr.state.il.us

INVASIVE SPECIES

While many introduced species have great recreational value, such as Brown Trout, many exotic species have caused problems. Never move fish, water or vegetation from one lake or stream to another, and always follow state laws. Details are available at the Illinois Department of Natural Resources website, www.dnr.state.il.us

FUN WITH FISH

There are many ways to enjoy Illinois' fish, from reading about them in this book to watching them in the wild. Hands-on activities are also popular. Many resident and nonresident anglers enjoy pursuing Illinois' game fish. The sport offers a great chance to enjoy the outdoors with friends and family, and in many cases, bring home a healthy meal of fresh fish.

Proceeds from license sales, along with special taxes anglers pay on fishing supplies and motorboat fuel, fund the majority of fish management efforts, including fish surveys, the development of special regulations and stocking programs. The sport also has a huge impact on Illinois' economy, supporting thousands of jobs in fishing, tourism and related industries.

CATCH-AND-RELEASE FISHING

Selective harvest (keeping some fish to eat and releasing the rest) and total catch-and-release fishing allow anglers to enjoy the sport without harming the resource. Catch-and-release is especially important with certain species and sizes of fish, and in lakes or rivers where biologists are trying to improve the fishery by protecting large predators or breeding age, adult fish. The fishing regulations, Illinois Department of Conservation website and your local fisheries' office are excellent sources of advice on which fish to keep and which to release.

Catch-and-release is only truly successful if the fish survives the experience. Following are helpful tips to reduce the chances of post-release mortality.

- Play and land fish quickly.

- Wet your hands before touching a fish to avoid removing its protective slime coating.

- Handle the fish gently and keep it in the water as much as possible.

- Do not hold the fish by the eyes or gills. Hold it by the lower lip or under the gill plate—and support its belly.

- If a fish is deeply hooked, cut the line so at least an inch hangs outside the mouth. This helps the hook lie flush when the fish takes in food.

- Circle hooks may help reduce the number of deeply hooked fish.

- Avoid fishing in deep water unless you plan to keep your catch.

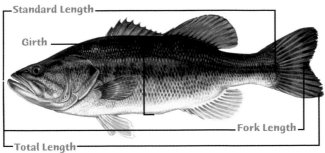

FISH MEASUREMENT

Fish are measured in three ways: standard length, fork length and total length. The first two are more accurate, because tails are often damaged or worn down. Total length is used in slot limits.

The following formulas estimate the weight of popular game fish. Lengths are in inches; weight is in pounds.

Formulas

Bass weight = (length x length x girth) / 1,200
Pike weight = (length x length x length) / 3,500
Sunfish weight = (length x length x length) / 1,200
Trout weight = (length x girth x girth) / 800
Walleye weight = (length x length x length) / 2,700

For example, let's say that you catch a 16-inch Walleye. Using the formula for Walleyes above: (16 x 16 x 16) divided by 2,700 = 1.5 pounds. Your Walleye would weigh approximately 1.5 pounds.

ILLINOIS MASTER ANGLER STATE RECORDS

Amended December 2006. The Illinois Record Fish List is updated by the Illinois Department of Natural Resources, and is available at: http://dnr.state.il.us/fish/

SPECIES	WEIGHT (LBS.-OZ.)	WHERE CAUGHT	YEAR
Bass, Largemouth	13-1	Stone Quarry Lake	1976
Bass, Rock	1-10	Aux Sable Creek	1987
Bass, Smallmouth	6-7	Strip Mine	1985
Bass, Hybrid Striped	20-0	Lake of Egypt	1993
Bass, Spotted	7-3	Strip Mine	1992
Bass, Striped	31-7	Sangchris Lake	1994
Bass, White	4-14	Kaskaskia River	1981
Bass, Yellow	2-0	Farm Pond	1994
Bluegill	3-8	Farm Pond	1987
Bowfin	16-6	Rend Lake	1984
Buffalo	48-0	Mississippi River	1936
Buffalo, Black	23-12	Rock River	1984
Bullhead, Black	5-6	Strip Mine	1988
Bullhead, Brown	2-10	Weldon Springs	1993
Bullhead, Yellow	5-4	Fox River	1955
Carp, Bighead	43	Lyerla Lake	1995
Carp, Common	51	Lake Hillcrest	1994
Carp, Grass	69-8	Lake Petersburg	2000
Catfish, Blue	85	Mississippi River	2000
Catfish, Channel	45-4	Baldwin Lake	1987
Catfish, Flathead	78-0	Carlyle Lake	1995
Crappie, Black	4-7	Rend Lake	1976
Crappie, White	4-7	Farm Pond	1973
Drum, Freshwater	35-0	DuQuion City Lake	1960
Gar, Longnose	17-5	Kankakee River	2002
Gar, Shortnose	5-1	Vermillion River	1999
Gar, Spotted	17-13	Horseshoe Lake	2004
Goldeye	2-1	Embarras River	1998
Muskellunge	38-8	Kaskaskia River	2002
Muskellunge, Tiger	31-3	Lake Will	2004
Perch, Yellow	2-9	Arrowhead Club Lake	1974
Pike, Northern	26-15	Strip Mine Lake	1989

SPECIES	WEIGHT (LBS.-OZ.)	WHERE CAUGHT	YEAR
Redhorse, Shorthead	2-3	Spoon River	2003
Redhorse, Silver	5-10	Fox River	2003
Salmon, Atlantic	18-11	Lake Michigan	1979
Salmon, Chinook	37-0	Lake Michigan	1976
Salmon, Coho	29-9	Lake Michigan	1972
Salmon, Pink	3-4	Lake Michigan	1992
Sauger	5-13	Mississippi River	1967
Saugeye	9-11	Evergreen Lake	2001
Sturgeon, Shovelnose	8-6	Rock River	2003
Sunfish, Green	2-1	Farm Pond	1981
Sunfish, Hybrid	2-5	Farm Pond	1990
Sunfish, Redear	2-12	Marion CC Lake	1985
Trout, Brook	7-5	Lake Michigan	1998
Trout, Brown	36-12	Lake Michigan	1997
Trout, Lake	38-4	Lake Michigan	1999
Trout, Rainbow	31-7	Lake Michigan	1993
Trout, Tiger	80-13	Lake Michigan	1977
Walleye	14-0	Kankakee River	1961
Warmouth	1-13	Farm Pond	1971

FISH CONSUMPTION ADVISORIES

Most fish are safe to eat, but pollutants in the food chain are a valid concern. The Illinois Department of Conservation routinely monitors contaminant levels in fish and wildlife, and the state Department of Public Health (IDPH) issues an advisory on eating sport fish and wildlife taken in Illinois because some of these foods contain potentially harmful levels of chemical contaminants. Advisory information can be found on the IDPH website, www.idph.state or by calling (800) 782-7860.

These pages explain how the information is presented for each fish.

SAMPLE FISH ILLUSTRATION

Description: brief summary of physical characteristics to help you identify the fish, such as coloration and markings, body shape, fin size and placement

Similar Species: lists other fish that look similar and the pages on which they can be found; also includes detailed inset drawings (below) highlighting physical traits such as markings, mouth size or shape and fin characteristics to help you distinguish this fish from similar species

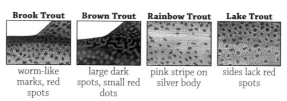

Brook Trout	Brown Trout	Rainbow Trout	Lake Trout
worm-like marks, red spots	large dark spots, small red dots	pink stripe on silver body	sides lack red spots

SAMPLE COMPARE ILLUSTRATIONS

COMMON NAME
Scientific Name

Other Names: common terms or nicknames you may hear to describe this species

Habitat: environment where the fish is found (such as streams, rivers, small or large lakes, fast-flowing or still water, in or around vegetation, near shore, in clear water)

Range: geographic distribution, starting with the fish's over-all range, followed by state-specific information

Food: what the fish eats most of the time (such as crustaceans, insects, fish, plankton)

Reproduction: timing of and behavior during the spawning period (dates and water temperatures, migration information, preferred spawning habitat, type of nest if applicable, colonial or solitary nester, parental care for eggs or fry)

Average Size: average length or range of length, average weight or range of weight

Records: state—the state record for this species, location and year; North American—the North American record for this species, location and year (based on the Fresh Water Fishing Hall of Fame)

Notes: Interesting natural history information. This can include unique behaviors, remarkable features, sporting and table quality, details on migrations, seasonal patterns or population trends.

Description: brownish-green back and sides with white belly; long, stout body; rounded tail; continuous dorsal fin; bony plates covering head; males have a large "eye" spot at the base of the tail

Similar Species: American Eel (pg. 46), Burbot (pg. 42), Sea Lamprey (pg. 66)

Bowfin	**American Eel**	**Burbot**
one dorsal fin, short anal fin	fused dorsal, tail and anal fin	two dorsals, long anal fin

Bowfin	**Burbot**	**Sea Lamprey**
no barbel on chin	small barbel on chin	mouth is a sucking disk

BOWFIN
Amia calva

Amiidae

Other Names: dogfish, grindle, mudfish, cypress trout, lake lawyer, beaverfish

Habitat: deep waters associated with vegetation in warmwater lakes and rivers; feeds in shallow weedbeds

Range: Mississippi river drainage east through the St. Lawrence drainage, south from Texas to Florida; southern half of Illinois

Food: fish, crayfish

Reproduction: in spring when water exceeds 61 degrees, male removes vegetation to build a two-foot nest in sand or gravel; one or more females deposit up to 5,000 eggs in nest; male tenaciously guards the nest and "ball" of young

Average Size: 12 to 24 inches, 2 to 5 pounds

Records: State—16 pounds, 6 ounces, Bay Creek, Pope County, 1992; North American—21 pounds, 8 ounces, Forest Lake, South Carolina, 1980

Notes: A voracious predator, the Bowfin prowls shallow weedbeds preying on anything that moves. Once thought detrimental to game fish populations, it is now considered an asset in controlling rough fish and stunted game fish. Air breathers that tolerate low oxygen levels, Bowfins can survive buried in mud for short periods during drought conditions. As more wetlands are drained, the shallow, weedy ponds preferred by Bowfins are disappearing and their numbers are decreasing. Not considered a game fish in Illinois.

Description: black to olive-green back; sides yellowish-green; belly creamy white to yellow; light bar at base of tail; barbels around mouth dark at base; adipose fin; lacks scales; round tail

Similar Species: Brown Bullhead (pg. 28), Flathead Catfish (pg. 36), Madtom/Stonecat (pg. 40), White Catfish (pg. 38), Yellow Bullhead (pg. 30)

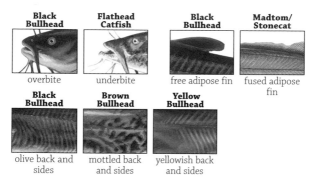

Black Bullhead	**Flathead Catfish**	**Black Bullhead**	**Madtom/ Stonecat**
overbite	underbite	free adipose fin	fused adipose fin

Black Bullhead	**Brown Bullhead**	**Yellow Bullhead**
olive back and sides	mottled back and sides	yellowish back and sides

BLACK BULLHEAD

Ameiurus melas

Other Names: common bullhead, horned pout

Habitat: shallow, slow-moving streams and backwaters; lakes and ponds—tolerates extremely turbid (cloudy) conditions

Range: Southern Canada through the Great Lakes and the Mississippi River watershed to the Southwest and into Mexico; Illinois—common throughout the state

Food: a scavenging opportunist; feeds mostly on animal material (dead or alive) but will eat plant matter

Reproduction: spawns from late April to early June; builds nest in shallow water with a muddy bottom; both sexes guard nest, eggs and young to 1 inch in size

Average Size: 8 to 10 inches, 4 ounces to 1 pound

Records: State—5 pounds, 6 ounces, Strip Mine, Fulton County, 1988; North American—8 pounds, 15 ounces, Sturgis Pond, Michigan, 1987

Notes: The Black Bullhead is the most widespread and common of the bullhead species in Illinois. It is also the bullhead species most tolerant of silt, pollution and low oxygen levels, but its numbers have decreased since the early twentieth century. As table fare, bullheads get little respect, but they are bigger than most panfish taken home to eat, and as tasty too.

Description: yellowish-brown upper body, with mottling on back and sides; barbels around mouth; adipose fin; scaleless skin; rounded tail; well-defined barbs on the pectoral spines

Similar Species: Black Bullhead (pg. 26), Flathead Catfish (pg. 36), Madtom/Stonecat (pg. 40), White Catfish (pg. 38), Yellow Bullhead (pg. 30)

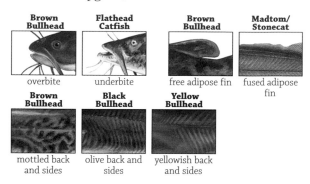

Brown Bullhead	Flathead Catfish	Brown Bullhead	Madtom/ Stonecat
overbite	underbite	free adipose fin	fused adipose fin

Brown Bullhead	Black Bullhead	Yellow Bullhead
mottled back and sides	olive back and sides	yellowish back and sides

BROWN BULLHEAD

Ameiurus nebulosus

Other Names: marbled or speckled bullhead, red cat

Habitat: warm, weedy lakes and sluggish streams

Range: Southern Canada through the Great Lakes down the eastern states to Florida, introduced in the West; Illinois—northeast, and flood plains of Illinois River

Food: scavenging opportunist feeding mostly on insects, fish, fish eggs, snails, some plant matter

Reproduction: in early summer, male builds nest in shallow water with vegetation with a sand or rocky bottom; both sexes guard the eggs and young

Average Size: 8 to 10 inches, 4 ounces to 2 pounds

Records: State—2 pounds, 10 ounces, Weldon Springs, Dewitt County, 1993; North American—6 pounds, 2 ounces, Pearl River, Mississippi, 1991

Notes: The Brown Bullhead is the second most abundant bullhead in Illinois and the smallest and can be found in turbid backwaters as well as in clear lakes. Adults are very involved in rearing their young, first by agitating the eggs then guarding the fry until they grow to about one inch long. The young are black and can often be seen swimming in a tight, swarming ball. Like other catfish, bullheads are nocturnal feeders. The Brown Bullhead is not highly pursued by anglers, though its reddish meat is tasty and fine table fare.

Description: olive head and back; yellowish-green head and sides; white belly; barbels on lower jaw are pale green or white; adipose fin; scaleless skin; rounded tail

Similar Species: Black Bullhead (pg. 26), Brown Bullhead (pg. 28), Flathead Catfish (pg. 36), Madtom/Stonecat (pg. 40)

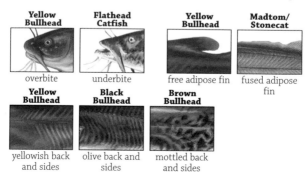

Yellow Bullhead — overbite

Flathead Catfish — underbite

Yellow Bullhead — free adipose fin

Madtom/Stonecat — fused adipose fin

Yellow Bullhead — yellowish back and sides

Black Bullhead — olive back and sides

Brown Bullhead — mottled back and sides

YELLOW BULLHEAD

Ameiurus natalis

Other Names: white-whiskered bullhead, yellow cat

Habitat: well-vegetated, warm lakes and sluggish streams

Range: southern Great Lakes through the eastern half of the U.S. to the Gulf and into Mexico, introduced in the West; in Illinois, common throughout the state

Food: scavenging opportunist, feeds on insects, crayfish, snails, small fish and plant material

Reproduction: in late spring to early summer, males build nest in shallow water with some vegetation and a soft bottom; both sexes guard the eggs and young

Average Size: 8 to 10 inches, 1 to 2 pounds

Records: State—5 pounds, 4 ounces, Fox River, Kane County, 1955 (not recognized as the national record); North American—4 pounds, 15 ounces, Ogeechee River, Georgia, 2003

Notes: The Yellow Bullhead is the bullhead species least tolerant of turbidity and prefers streams, but it will occupy ponds if they are reasonably clear. Bullheads feed by "taste," locating food by following chemical trails through the water. This ability can be greatly diminished in polluted water, impairing their ability to find food. The Yellow Bullhead is less likely than other bullhead species to overpopulate a lake and become stunted.

Description: pale blue back and sides, large fish may be dark bluish-gray; white belly; no spots; forked tail; anal fin straight on rear edge; eyes appear to be located on lower half of head; adipose fin; long barbels around mouth

Similar Species: Channel Catfish (pg. 34), White Catfish (pg. 38)

Blue Catfish	Channel Catfish	White Catfish
30 to 36 rays in anal fin, no spots, straight edged anal fin	24 to 29 rays in anal fin, spots, curved anal fin	19 to 23 rays in anal fin, no spots, curved anal fin

BLUE CATFISH
Ictalurus furcatus

Other Names: white, silver, Mississippi or river cat

Habitat: swift current or deep flowing pools of large rivers, large impoundments, stocked in smaller impoundments for specialized fishing

Range: Mississippi and Ohio River drainage in central U.S, introduced in the West; in Illinois, common in the Mississippi River south of the Missouri River, infrequent in the upper Ohio and Illinois Rivers

Food: small fish, often dead or injured shad

Reproduction: adults mature at 4 to 6 years; spawning occurs in sheltered areas at the edge of currents, often in cavities or behind rocks; eggs and fry are guarded by adults

Average Size: 2 to 3 feet, 20 to 40 pounds

Records: State—85 pounds, Mississippi River, Alexander County, 2000; North American—121 pounds, 8 ounces, Lake Texoma, Texas, 2004

Notes: The Blue Catfish is the largest U.S. catfish. They occupy the fast water of large rivers, and were widespread in the central states before these rivers were dammed. Blue Catfish often suspend 20 feet off the bottom, below large schools of shad, while the largest fish frequently congregate below dams where they feed on injured fish passing through the turbines or over spillways.

Description: steel gray to silver on the back and sides; white belly; black spots on the sides; large fish lack spots and appear dark olive or slate; forked tail; adipose fin; long barbels around mouth

Similar Species: Bullheads (pp. 26-31), White Catfish (pg. 38)

Channel Catfish

deeply forked tail

Bullheads

tail rounded or slightly notched

Channel Catfish

24 to 30 rays in anal fin, spots

White Catfish

19 to 23 rays in anal fin, no spots

CHANNEL CATFISH

Ictalurus punctatus

Ictaluridae

Other Names: spotted, speckled or silver catfish

Habitat: prefers clean, fast-moving streams with deep pools; stocked in many lakes; can tolerate turbid (cloudy) waters

Range: southern Canada through the Midwest to the Gulf of Mexico into Mexico and Florida, introduced throughout much of the United States; in Illinois, common throughout the state

Food: insects, crustaceans, fish, some plant debris

Reproduction: in early summer, male builds nest in dark, sheltered area such as an undercut bank or log; female deposits gelatinous eggs; male guards the eggs and young until the nest is deserted

Average Size: 12 to 20 inches, 3 to 4 pounds

Records: State—45 pounds, 4 ounces, Baldwin Lake, St. Clair County, 1987; North American—58 pounds, Santee Cooper Reservoir, South Carolina, 1964

Notes: This highly respected sport fish is becoming less common in central Illinois, probably due to increased turbidity and extreme low water levels during droughts. They are still abundant in the Mississippi and its tributaries. Like other catfish, Channel Catfish are nocturnal and are most successfully fished for at night; they put up a strong fight and are fine table fare. They were the first widely farmed fish in the U.S. and are now common in grocery stores and restaurants throughout the country.

Description: color variable, usually mottled yellow or brown; belly cream to yellow; adipose fin; chin barbels; lacks scales; tail squared; head broad and flattened; pronounced underbite

Similar Species: Bullheads (pp. 26-31), Channel Catfish (pg. 34), White Catfish (pg. 38)

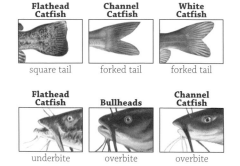

Flathead Catfish	Channel Catfish	White Catfish
square tail	forked tail	forked tail

Flathead Catfish	Bullheads	Channel Catfish
underbite	overbite	overbite

FLATHEAD CATFISH
Pylodictis olivaris

Other Names: shovelnose, shovelhead; yellow, mud, pied or Mississippi cat

Habitat: deep pools of large rivers and impoundments

Range: the Mississippi River watershed and into Mexico, large rivers in the Southwest; in Illinois, common in large rivers and impoundments throughout the state except in the northeast

Food: fish, crayfish

Reproduction: spawns when water is 72 to 80 degrees; male builds and defends nest in hollow log, undercut bank or other sheltered area; large females may lay up to 30,000 eggs

Average Size: 20 to 30 inches, 10 to 20 pounds

Records: State—78 pounds, Carlyle Lake, Clinton County, 1995; North American—123 pounds, Elk River Reservoir, Kansas, 1998

Notes: The Flathead Catfish is a solitary predator that feeds aggressively on live fish, often at night. It is frequently found near logjams or in deep pools. A tenacious fighter, it is known for its firm, white flesh. Flatheads have been introduced into a few lakes in an attempt to control stunted panfish populations.

Description: bluish-silver body and off-white belly; older
fish dark blue with some mottling; forked tail with pointed
lobes; lacks scales; adipose fin; white chin barbels

Similar Species: Bullheads (pp. 26-31), Channel Catfish (pg. 34)

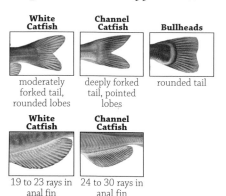

White Catfish
moderately
forked tail,
rounded lobes

Channel Catfish
deeply forked
tail, pointed
lobes

Bullheads
rounded tail

White Catfish
19 to 23 rays in
anal fin

Channel Catfish
24 to 30 rays in
anal fin

WHITE CATFISH

Ameiurus catus

Ictaluridae

Other Names: whitey, silver or weed catfish

Habitat: freshwater and slightly brackish water in coastal streams and lakes

Range: Maine south to Florida and west to Texas; introduced in some western states; in Illinois, fee-fishing lakes, the Mississippi, Illinois, and Kaskaskie Rivers

Food: insects, crayfish, small fish, and plant debris

Reproduction: male builds nest in sheltered area with a sand or gravel bottom when water temperatures reach the high 60s; both sexes guard nest and eggs until fry disperse

Average Size: 10 to 18 inches, 1 to 2 pounds

Records: State—none; North American—22 pounds, William Land Park Pond, California, 1994

Notes: The White Catfish is not native to Illinois but was introduced to stock fee-fishing lakes and now has become established in some rivers. In terms of habits, White Catfish prefer quieter water than Channel Catfish with a somewhat firmer bottom than that sought by bullheads. They frequent the edge of reedbeds and are often caught when still-fishing the bottom near deep water. White Catfish are not considered a prized sport fish, but they have firm flesh and fine flavor.

STONECAT

TADPOLE MADTOM

Description: Tadpole Madtom—dark olive to brown; dark line on side; large, fleshy head; Stonecat—similar but lacks dark stripe, and has protruding upper jaw; both species have an adipose fin continuous with tail

Similar Species: Bullheads (pp. 26-31), Catfish (pp. 32-39)

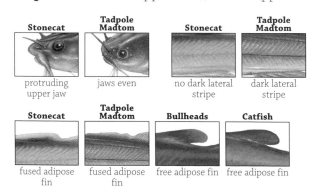

Stonecat	Tadpole Madtom	Stonecat	Tadpole Madtom
protruding upper jaw	jaws even	no dark lateral stripe	dark lateral stripe

Stonecat	Tadpole Madtom	Bullheads	Catfish
fused adipose fin	fused adipose fin	free adipose fin	free adipose fin

STONECAT *Noturus flavus*
TADPOLE MADTOM *Noturus gyrinus*

Other Name: willow cat

Habitat: vegetated water near shore in medium to large lakes, under rocks in stream riffles

Range: the eastern U.S.; in Illinois, Tadpole Madtom are common throughout the state, Stonecat prevalent in the northern half of the state

Food: small invertebrates, algae and other plant matter

Reproduction: spawn in late spring; female lays eggs under objects such as roots, rocks, logs or in abandoned crayfish burrows; eggs guarded by one parent

Average Size: Tadpole Madtom —3 to 4 inches; Stonecat—4 to 6 inches

Records: none

Notes: Small, secretive fish most active at night. Both species have poison glands under the skin at the base of the dorsal and pectoral fins. Though not lethal, the poison produces a painful burning sensation, reputed to bring even the hardiest anglers to their knees, if only for a short time. Stonecats, and to a lesser extent madtoms, are a common baitfish in some areas. Reportedly, damaging the "slime" coating (by rolling them in sand) to make handling easier will reduce their effectiveness as bait.

Description: mottled brown with creamy chin and belly; eel-like body; small barbel at each nostril opening; longer barbel on chin; long dorsal fin similar to and just above anal fin

Similar Species: American Eel (pg. 46), Bowfin (pg. 24), Sea Lamprey (pg. 66)

Burbot	**American Eel**	**Bowfin**
two dorsals, long anal fin	fused dorsal, tail and anal fin	one dorsal fin, short anal fin

Burbot	**Bowfin**	**Sea Lamprey**
small barbel on chin	no barbel on chin	mouth is a sucking disk

42

BURBOT
Lota lota

Other Names: lawyer, eelpout, ling, cusk

Habitat: deep, cold, clear, rock-bottomed lakes and streams

Range: northern North America into Siberia and across northern Europe; in Illinois, Lake Michigan and few specimens from Mississippi, Illinois and Big Muddy Rivers

Food: primarily small fish, but renowned for attempting to eat almost anything, including fish eggs, clams and crayfish

Reproduction: pairs to large groups spawn together in mid- to late winter under the ice, over a sand or gravel bottom in less than 15 feet of water; after spawning, thrashing adults scatter fertilized eggs; no nest is built and there is no parental care

Average Size: 20 inches, 2 to 8 pounds

Records: State—none; North American—22 pounds, 8 ounces, Little Athapapuskow Lake, Manitoba, 1994

Notes: The Burbot is a coldwater fish, seldom found in fisheries where the water temperature routinely exceeds 69 degrees. It is popular with ice fisherman in some western states and Scandinavia. Despite its firm, white good-tasting flesh, it is considered a nuisance fish in Illinois, particularly in Lake Michigan.

Description: gray back with purple or bronze reflections; silver sides; white underbelly; humped back; dorsal fin extends from hump to near tail; lateral line runs from head through the tail

Similar Species: White Bass (pg. 186)

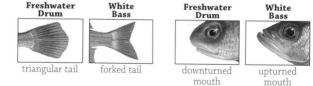

Freshwater Drum	White Bass	Freshwater Drum	White Bass
triangular tail	forked tail	downturned mouth	upturned mouth

FRESHWATER DRUM

Sciaenidae

Aplodinotus grunniens

Other Names: sheepshead, croaker, thunderpumper, grinder, bubbler (commercially marketed as white perch)

Habitat: slow-to moderate current areas of rivers and streams; shallow lakes with soft bottoms; prefers turbid (cloudy) water

Range: Canada south through Midwest into eastern Mexico to Guatemala; in Illinois, common in all larger rivers, less frequent in smaller streams, extirpated from southern Lake Michigan

Food: small fish, insects, crayfish, clams

Reproduction: in May and June after water temperatures reach about 66 degrees, schools of drum lay eggs near the surface in open water, over sand or gravel; no parental care of fry

Average Size: 10 to 14 inches, 2 to 5 pounds

Records: State—35 pounds, DuQuoin City Lake, Perry County, 1960; North American—54 pounds, 8 ounces, Nickajack Lake, Tennessee, 1972

Notes: The only freshwater member of a large family of marine fish. Drums are named for a grunting noise that is made by males, primarily to attract females. The sound is produced when specialized muscles rub along the swim bladder. The skull contains two enlarged L-shaped earstones called otoliths, once prized for jewelry by Native Americans. The flesh is flaky, white and tasty but easily dries out when cooked, due to the low oil content.

45

Description: dark brown on top with yellow sides and white belly; long snake-like body with large mouth, pectoral fins and gill slits; a continuous dorsal, tail and anal fin

Similar Species: Bowfin (pg. 24), Burbot (pg. 42), Sea Lamprey (pg. 66)

American Eel	**Bowfin**	**Burbot**
fused dorsal, tail and anal fin	one dorsal fin, short anal fin	two dorsals, long anal fin

American Eel	**Sea Lamprey**
mouth has jaws	mouth is a sucking disk

AMERICAN EEL

Anguilla rostrata

Other Names: common, Boston, Atlantic or freshwater eel

Habitat: soft bottoms of medium to large streams, brackish tidewater areas

Range: the Atlantic Ocean; eastern and central North America and eastern Central America; in Illinois, once common throughout the state but now rare

Food: insects, crayfish, small fish

Reproduction: a "catadromous" species, it spends most of its life in freshwater, returning to the Sargasso Sea in the North Atlantic Ocean to spawn; females lay up to 20 million eggs; adults die after spawning

Average Size: 24 to 36 inches, 1 to 3 pounds

Records: State—none;   North American—8 pounds, 8 ounces, Cliff Pond, Massachusetts, 1992

Notes: Leaf-shaped larval eels drift with ocean currents for about a year. When they reach river mouths of North and Central America, they morph into small eels (elvers). Males remain in the estuaries; females migrate upstream. At maturity (up to 20 years of age) adults return to the Sargasso Sea. Before settlement, eels commonly migrated up the Mississippi River to Illinois; with the many dams now in place, few eels reach this far inland. Nevertheless, after the opening of the Welland Canal, eels entered the Great Lakes from the Atlantic.

Description: olive to brown with dark spots along sides; long, cylindrical profile; single dorsal fin located just above the anal fin; body is encased in hard, plate-like scales; snout twice as long as head; needle-sharp teeth on both jaws

Similar Species: Shortnose Gar (pg. 50), Spotted Gar (pg. 52)

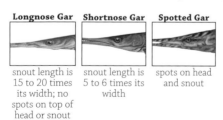

Longnose Gar	**Shortnose Gar**	**Spotted Gar**
snout length is 15 to 20 times its width; no spots on top of head or snout	snout length is 5 to 6 times its width	spots on head and snout

LONGNOSE GAR

Lepisosteus osseus

Other Names: garfish

Habitat: quiet waters of larger rivers and lakes

Range: central United States throughout the Mississippi drainage south into Mexico, a few rivers in the northeast in the Great Lakes drainage; in Illinois, common statewide

Food: minnows and other small fish

Reproduction: lays large, green eggs in weedy shallows when water temperatures reach the high 60s; using a small disk on the snout, a newly-hatched gar attaches to nearby plants, rocks or branches until its digestive tract develops enough to begin feeding

Average Size: 1 to 3 feet, 2 to 5 pounds

Records: State—17 pounds, 5 ounces, Kankakee River, Grundy County, 2002; North American—50 pounds, 5 ounces, Trinity River, Texas, 1954

Notes: The Longnose Gar belongs to a prehistoric family of fish that can breathe air with the aid of a modified swim bladder. This adaptation makes them well-suited to survive in increasingly polluted rivers and lakes. They hunt by floating motionless near the surface then make a swift, sideways slash to capture prey; it is a valuable asset in controlling the increasing populations of rough fish. Gar are not often sought by anglers, but are frequently the target of bow fishermen.

Description: head, back and sides olive to slate green; long cylindrical body; single dorsal fin located just above the anal fin; body encased in hard plate-like scales; snout a third longer than its head; needle-sharp teeth on both jaws

Similar Species: Longnose Gar (pg. 48), Spotted Gar (pg. 52)

Shortnose Gar	**Longnose Gar**	**Spotted Gar**
snout length is about 6 times its width	snout length is about 15 to 20 times its width	spots on head and snout

SHORTNOSE GAR

Lepisosteus platostomas

Other Names: stubnose, broadnose or shortbilled gar

Habitat: open water of warm, slow-moving streams, backwaters and shallow oxbow lakes

Range: the Mississippi River drainage from the southern Great Lakes to Mexico; in Illinois, very abundant in the Mississippi, Illinois and Ohio Rivers and their large tributaries and floodplain lakes

Food: minnows and small fish, crayfish

Reproduction: spawns in weedy backwaters when water temperatures reach the mid-60s; the large, yellowish-green eggs are poisonous to mammals

Average Size: 1 to 2 feet, 1 to 3 pounds

Records: State—5 pounds, 1 ounce, Vermilion River, LaSalle County, 1999; North American—6 pounds, 6 ounces, Kentucky Lake, Tennessee, 2001

Notes: The Shortnose Gar is smaller and less common in Illinois than the Longnose Gar. It prefers somewhat more active water and can tolerate more turbidity than other gars. Like other gars, it can "gulp" air and withstand very warm and poorly oxygenated water. It is an ambush hunter and is frequently seen floating near brush piles at the current's edge. It has a strong fishy flavor and is not often sought by anglers.

Description: olive back and sides; spots on entire body including snout, fins, and tail; cylindrical body; narrow snout slightly longer than the head; sharp teeth on both jaws

Similar Species: Longnose Gar (pg. 48), Shortnose Gar (pg. 50)

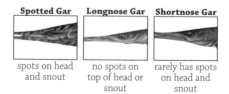

Spotted Gar	Longnose Gar	Shortnose Gar
spots on head and snout	no spots on top of head or snout	rarely has spots on head and snout

SPOTTED GAR

Lepisosteus oculatus

Lepisosteidae

Other Names: speckled gar

Habitat: quiet, clear, weedy water in streams and lakes

Range: southern Great Lakes Basin southeast to Florida; in Illinois, the Green, Illinois and southern Mississippi Rivers, uncommon in Lake Michigan

Food: minnows, small fish, and insects

Reproduction: spawns in weedy backwaters when water temperatures reach the mid-60s; adhesive eggs are scattered over vegetation, algae mats or standing timber; no parental care

Average Size: 1 to 2 feet, 1 to 2 pounds

Records: State—7 pounds, 13 ounces, Horseshoe Lake, Alexander County, 2004; North American—50 pounds, 5 ounces, Trinity River, Texas, 1954

Notes: The Spotted Gar is the smallest gar in Illinois, and the species that requires the clearest water and the most vegetation. With increased runoff, many streams are becoming too turbid (cloudy) for this small gar. Like other gars, it can breathe air with the help of a modified swim bladder; it can therefore tolerate very warm, poorly oxygenated water. The Spotted Gar is a fun aquarium fish and is often sold in pet shops, but it requires live food to do well.

Description: dark gray body with black or brown blotches; divided dorsal fin with green border; black spot at base of front dorsal fin; pelvic fin fused to form sucker-like disk; large head with a rapidly tapering body

Similar Species: Mottled Sculpin (pg. 130)

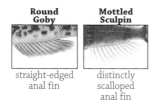

Round Goby — straight-edged anal fin

Mottled Sculpin — distinctly scalloped anal fin

ROUND GOBY
Neogobius melanostomus

Other Names: ship or tank goby

Habitat: bottom dweller of rocky or weedy shorelines in large, clear lakes; favors deep water during winter

Range: native to the Black and Caspian Sea; in Illinois, present in Lake Michigan

Food: mollusks, crustaceans, fish eggs, small fish

Reproduction: spawns from late spring through early summer; males spread a sticky substance on the undersides of logs or rocks, on which females attach eggs; several females may use the same nest; males guard the nests and may die after spawning season

Average Size: 4 to 5 inches

Records: none

Notes: A secretive fish that hides under rocks or buries itself in sand, the Round Goby is an invasive species that was transported from Eurasia in ballast water of oceangoing ships. A voracious feeder and a prolific breeder, Gobies are spreading rapidly and threatening native species. The only benefit of this species is that it can consume 30 to 50 Zebra Mussels in a day.

Description: blue to blue-green metallic back; silver sides with faint dark stripes; white belly; purple spot just behind the gill and above the pectoral fin; large mouth with protruding lower jaw; sharply pointed scales (scutes) along the ventral midline

Similar Species: Gizzard Shad (pg. 60), Skipjack Herring (pg. 58)

Alewife	**Gizzard Shad**	**Alewife**	**Skipjack Herring**
lower jaw protruding beyond snout	snout protruding over mouth	purple spot behind upper edge of gill	no spot behind upper edge of gill
Alewife	**Gizzard Shad**	**Alewife**	**Skipjack Herring**
no long thread on last ray of dorsal fin	last ray of dorsal fin extending into long thread	back gray-green back, shades gradually to silver sides	blue-green back ends abruptly at silver sides

ALEWIFE
Alosa pseudoharengus

Other Names: ellwife, sawbelly, golden shad, big-eyed herring, river herring

Habitat: open water of the Great Lakes and a few inland lakes

Range: the Atlantic Ocean from Labrador to the Carolinas, the St. Lawrence River drainage and the Great Lakes; in Illinois, Lake Michigan

Food: zooplankton, filamentous algae

Reproduction: in the Great Lakes, spawning takes place in open water of bays and along protected shorelines during early summer

Average Size: 4 to 8 inches

Records: none

Notes: Alewives were first seen in Lake Ontario in the 1870s and may be native there. Soon after the completion of the Welland Canal in the 1930s, they spread to the other Great Lakes, reaching Lake Michigan in 1949. With the introduction of the Sea Lamprey and the subsequent decline of the Lake Trout, the Alewife population grew exponentially. Today, with the Sea Lamprey under control and the recovery of the Lake Trout, Alewife population growth has moderated, and it has become the base for the Great Lakes sport fishery. Alewives are not well-suited to freshwater impoundments and occasionally experience late summer die-offs and wash up on the shore, to the disgust of beachgoers.

Description: deep, laterally compressed silver body with a blue-green back that ends abruptly; no dark spots on shoulder; sharply pointed scales along belly (scutes)

Similar Species: Alewife (pg. 56), Gizzard Shad (pg. 60)

Skipjack Herring	**Alewife**	**Skipjack Herring**	**Gizzard Shad**
blue-green back ends abruptly at silver sides	gray-green back shades to silver sides	no long thread on last ray of dorsal fin	long thread on last dorsal ray

Skipjack Herring	**Alewife**	**Skipjack Herring**	**Gizzard Shad**
no spot behind upper gill edge	dark spot behind upper gill edge	lower jaw protrudes beyond snout	snout protruding over mouth

SKIPJACK HERRING

Alosa chrysochloris

Other Names: river herring, skipper

Habitat: clear water in large rivers, often at the mouth of tributary streams and below dams

Range: Gulf Coast waters from Texas to Florida, the Mississippi River, its large tributaries and impoundments; in Illinois, occasionally in the Illinois River, and the Mississippi River below pool 25, common in the Ohio and Wabash Rivers

Food: small fish, insects

Reproduction: little is known about its spawning habits, but seems to spawn in early spring as individuals or in small schools in clear water near the mouth of tributary streams

Average Size: 12 to 16 inches, 1 to 2 pounds

Records: State—none;   North American—3 pounds, 12 ounces, White Bear Lake, Tennessee, 1982

Notes: The Skipjack Herring is a very fast fish that gets its name from the spectacular leaps out of the water it makes as it chases prey. Skipjacks are fish of the big rivers, and don't often enter smaller tributaries. They feed at the surface and prefer the clear, less turbid (cloudy) parts of the river. Skipjacks readily take flies and small lures and on light tackle are one of Illinois' best fighters.

Description: deep laterally compressed body; silvery blue back with white sides and belly; young fish have a dark spot on shoulder behind the gill; small mouth; last rays of dorsal fin form a long thread

Similar Species: Alewife (pg. 56), Skipjack Herring (pg. 58), Threadfin Shad (pg. 62)

Gizzard Shad
spot behind upper edge of gill

Skipjack Herring
no spot behind upper edge of gill

Gizzard Shad
last ray of dorsal fin extends into a thread

Alewife
last ray of dorsal fin doesn't extend a thread

Gizzard Shad
snout extends past mouth

Alewife
lower jaw extends beyond snout

Threadfin Shad
terminal mouth

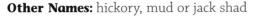

GIZZARD SHAD

Dorosoma cepedianum

Other Names: hickory, mud or jack shad

Habitat: large rivers, reservoirs, lakes, swamps and temporarily flooded pools; brackish and saline waters in coastal areas

Range: St. Lawrence and Great Lakes, Mississippi, Atlantic and Gulf Slope drainages from Quebec to Mexico, south to central Florida; common throughout Illinois

Food: herbivorous filter feeder

Reproduction: spawning takes place in tributary streams and along lakeshore in early summer; schooling adults release eggs in open water without regard for individual mates

Average Size: 6 to 8 inches, 1 to 8 ounces

Records: State—none; North American—4 pounds, 12 ounces, Lake Oahe, South Dakota, 2006

Notes: The Gizzard Shad is a widespread, prolific fish that is best known as forage for popular game fish. At times Gizzard Shad can become overabundant and experience large die-offs. The name "gizzard" refers to this shad's long, convoluted intestine that is often packed with sand. Though Gizzard Shad are a management problem at times, they form a valuable link in turning plankton into usable forage for large game fish. Occasionally, larger Gizzard Shad are caught with hook and line, but they have little food value.

Description: silvery yellow back with white sides and belly; dark spot on shoulder behind gill; deep laterally compressed body; small terminal mouth; last rays of dorsal fin form a long thread

Similar Species: Gizzard Shad (pg. 60)

Threadfin Shad	**Gizzard Shad**
terminal mouth	snout protrudes over mouth

Threadfin Shad	**Gizzard Shad**
yellow tail	no yellow on tail

THREADFIN SHAD

Dorosoma petenense

Other Names: silver, yellow or thread shad

Habitat: currents of warm large rivers and reservoirs; brackish and saline waters in coastal areas

Range: southern Mississippi River drainage through the Gulf states south into Central America; Illinois—Ohio and Wabasha Rivers

Food: herbivorous filter feeder

Reproduction: schools of shad spawn in the shallows along shore when water reaches the low 70s; adhesive eggs are spread over vegetation and left unguarded

Average Size: 2 to 5 inches

Records: none

Notes: The Threadfin Shad is similar to the Gizzard Shad but it is smaller and prefers currents in rivers and open water in reservoirs. It is a southern species that has spread into the central U.S. since the 1950s. It requires warm water and dies when water temperatures drop below 41 degrees. When the water warms in summer, they migrate upstream and can become very abundant in the lower Mississippi, Ohio and Wabash Rivers.

AMERICAN BROOK LAMPREY

Description: eel-like body; round, sucking-disk mouth; seven paired gill openings; dorsal fin long, extending to tail; no paired fins

Similar Species: American Eel (pg. 46), Sea Lamprey (pg. 66), Bowfin (pg. 24), Native Lampreys (pg. 64)

Native Lampreys

mouth is a sucking disk

Bowfin

mouth has jaws

American Eel

mouth has jaws

Native Lampreys

undivided dorsal fin

Sea Lamprey

dorsal divided by deep notch

NATIVE LAMPREYS

Petromyzontidae

Ichthyomyzon, Lampetra

Other Names: Ohio and silver lamprey, American brook, least brook, and northern brook lampreys

Habitat: juveniles live in the quiet pools of streams and rivers; adults may move into some lakes

Range: Mississippi and Ohio River drainages in central U.S; in Illinois, the Mississippi, Illinois, Ohio and Wabash Rivers

Food: juvenile lampreys are bottom dwellers and filter feeders in streams; adults are either parasitic on fish or do not feed

Reproduction: adults build nests in the gravel of streambeds when water temperatures reach the mid-50s, then die soon after spawning

Average Size: 6 to 12 inches

Records: none

Notes: Lampreys are some of Earth's oldest vertebrates, with fossil records dating back 500 million years. In Illinois, there are six native lampreys. The Ohio, Chestnut and Silver Lamprcys are parasitic in adult form, often leaving small round wounds on their prey. The Brook Lampreys are non-parasitic. All of the native lampreys coexist with the other Illinois fish species with little or no effect on their populations. Due to deteriorating water conditions, many native lampreys are endangered or threatened throughout their range.

Description: eel-like body; round, sucking-disk mouth; seven paired gill openings; long dorsal fin extends to tail and is divided into two parts by a deep notch; no paired fins

Similar Species: Sea Lamprey (pg. 66), American Eel (pg. 46), Bowfin (pg. 24)

Sea Lamprey

mouth is a sucking disk

American Eel

mouth has jaws

Bowfin

mouth has jaws

Sea Lamprey

dorsal fin divided by deep notch

Native Lampreys

undivided dorsal fin

SEA LAMPREY

Petromyzon marinus

Other Names: landlocked or lake lamprey

Habitat: juveniles live in quiet pools of freshwater streams; adults are free-swimming in lakes or oceans

Range: Atlantic Ocean from Greenland to Florida, Norway to the Mediterranean; in Illinois, Lake Michigan and associated spawning streams

Food: juveniles are filter feeders in freshwater streams; adults are parasitic and attach to fish with a disk-shaped sucker mouth, then use their sharp tongues to rasp through the scales and feed on blood and body fluids; many "host" fish die

Reproduction: adults build a nest in the gravel of clear streams, then die shortly after spawning; young remain in the streams several years before returning to lakes or the sea as adults

Average Size: 12 to 24 inches

Records: none

Notes: Native to eastern coastal streams of North America, with the completion of the Welland Canal in 1829, Sea Lampreys by passed Niagara Falls and entered the Great Lakes, reaching Lake Michigan in 1936. They had a devastating effect on native fish populations and the depleted Lake Trout and Whitefish populations soon collapsed. Today, Sea Lampreys are under partial control and Lake Trout populations have recovered enough to allow sport fishing and the Whitefish populations enough for moderate commercial fishing.

Description: olive green back and sides; scales outlined giving sides cross-hatched appearance; upturned mouth; dark bar under eye; rounded tail fin

Similar Species: Central Mudminnow (pg. 92), Fathead Minnow (pg. 84)

Mosquitofish	**Central Mudminnow**	**Fathead Minnow**
terminal mouth, bar under eye	mouth not upturned, no bar under eye	mouth not upturned, no bar under eye
Mosquitofish	**Central Mudminnow**	**Fathead Minnow**
female has spots on tail	rounded tail	forked tail

MOSQUITOFISH

Gambusia affinis

Other Names: mosquito or surface minnow

Habitat: surface of shallow, well-vegetated backwaters with little current

Range: southeastern U.S., introduced worldwide; in Illinois, common throughout the southeast

Food: insects, crustaceans and some plant material

Reproduction: gives birth to live young after internal fertilization; may produce several broods in a single season

Average Size: 2 to 3 inches

Records: none

Notes: There are few native livebearers in the U.S., but it is a well-represented family in the tropical and subtropical Americas. Male Mosquitofish use their modified anal fin to transfer sperm to the much larger females. Females can store sperm up to ten months and then give birth to live fry. Mosquitofish have been introduced worldwide to control mosquitoes but seem to be no better at pest control than native species. Mosquitofish have broad ecological tolerance and can survive high temperatures and salinity and low oxygen levels.

Description: dark gray to black back; silver-gray sides with dark blotches; low-set eyes; upturned mouth; tiny body scales, none on head

Similar Species: Common Carp (pg. 72), Grass Carp (pg. 74), Silver Carp (pg. 78)

Bighead Carp	**Silver Carp**	**Common Carp**	**Grass Carp**
keeled belly from pelvic fin to anal fin	keeled belly from throat to anal fin	large body scales	scales showing prominent dark edge

Bighead Carp	**Silver Carp**	**Common Carp**
upturned mouth lacks barbels, eyes low on head	upturned mouth lacks barbels, eyes low on head	downturned sucker mouth and barbels, eyes high up

BIGHEAD CARP

Hypophthalmichthys nobilis

Other Names: river carp, lake fish, speckled amur

Habitat: large, warm rivers and connected lakes

Range: Asia, introduced in other parts of the world; in Illinois, in the Mississippi and Ohio Rivers and larger tributaries

Food: aquatic vegetation and floating plankton, mostly algae

Reproduction: spawns from late spring to early summer in warm, flowing water

Average Size: 24 to 36 inches, 5 to 50 pounds

Records: State—45 pounds, 3 ounces, Lyerla Lake, Union Lake, 1995; North American—90 pounds, Kirby Lake, Texas, 2000

Notes: Bighead Carp are the fourth most important aquaculture fish in the world. They were introduced to the U.S. to control algae in southern aquaculture ponds and are now commonly farmed as a dual crop with catfish. They escaped to the Mississippi River and are now well established in the Ohio River and are the predominant fish in some areas. The Silver Carp, and to a lesser degree the Bighead Carp, makes high leaps from the water when frightened by boats. As filter feeders, Bighead Carp are targets for bow fishermen but not anglers. They have a pleasant, mild flavor, but are bony and are not highly regarded table fare in this country.

Description: brassy yellow to dark olive back and sides; whitish-yellow belly; round mouth has two pairs of barbels; reddish tail and anal fin; each scale has a dark margin

Similar Species: Bighead Carp (pg. 70), Grass Carp (pg. 74), Silver Carp (pg. 78)

Common Carp	Silver Carp	Grass Carp	Bighead Carp
large body scales	keeled belly from gills to anal fin	scales showing prominent dark edge	keeled belly from pelvic fin to anal fin

Common Carp	Bighead Carp	Silver Carp
downturned sucker mouth with barbels, eyes high up	upturned mouth lacks barbels, eyes low on head	upturned mouth lacks barbels, eyes low on head

COMMON CARP

Cyprinus carpio

Other Names: German, European, mirror or leather carp, buglemouth

Habitat: warm, shallow, quiet, well-vegetated waters of streams and lakes

Range: native to Asia, introduced throughout the world; in Illinois, common throughout the state

Food: opportunistic feeder; prefers insect larvae, crustaceans and mollusks, but at times eats algae and some higher plants

Reproduction: spawns from late spring to early summer in very shallow water at stream and lake edges; very obvious when spawning with a great deal of splashing

Average Size: 16 to 18 inches, 5 to 20 pounds

Records: State—51 pounds, Lake Hillcrest, Madison County 1994; North American—57 pounds, 13 ounces, Tidal Basin, Washington D.C., 1983

Notes: The carp is one of the world's most important freshwater fish. This fast-growing fish provides sport and food for millions of people throughout its range. This Asian minnow was introduced into Europe in the twelfth century but didn't make it to North America until the 1800s. Carp readily hybridize with Goldfish, and in polluted marginal habitat this hybrid can be the predominant fish. Carp are a highly prized sport fish in Europe, but they have not gained the same status in the U.S., even though some anglers and bowhunters actively fish for carp.

Description: olive to silver-white back; cross-hatched sides; large scales with a dark edge and a black spot; clear to gray-brown fins; upturned mouth; no barbels near mouth

Similar Species: Bighead Carp (pg. 70), Common Carp (pg. 72), Silver Carp (pg. 78)

Grass Carp

scales with a prominent dark edge

Bighead Carp

keeled belly from pelvic fin to anal fin

Silver Carp

keeled belly from gills to anal fin

Common Carp

large body scales

Grass Carp

mouth lacks barbels

Common Carp

downturned sucker mouth with barbels, eyes high up

GRASS CARP

Ctenopharyngodon idella

Other Names: white amur

Habitat: lakes, ponds and backwaters of large, warm rivers

Range: Asia, introduced in other parts of the world; in Illinois, the Mississippi and Ohio Rivers and larger tributaries, introduced in ponds and lakes throughout state

Food: submerged aquatic vegetation, some floating algae

Reproduction: spawns from late spring to early summer, laying over a million eggs in warm, slowly flowing water; eggs remain suspended for several days before hatching

Average Size: 18 to 30 inches; 5 to 30 pounds

Records: State—69 pound, 8 ounces, Lake Petersburg, Menard County, 2000; North American—80 pounds, Lake Wedington, Arkansas, 2004

Notes: Grass Carp were introduced into the U.S. in the 1960s for aquaculture and aquatic vegetation control. By the late '70s, Grass Carp could be found in 40 states. Using Grass Carp for vegetation control is still permitted and popular in many states, including Illinois, but only when using non-breeding (triploid) fish. Grass Carp are well-established in the lakes and streams of the Ohio River basin. They are more often hooked than the other Asian carp but not consistently enough to be of interest to anglers.

FERAL GOLDFISH

RELEASED GOLDFISH

Description: olive green, red, orange, gold or pink, variegated
black and orange; deep body, fins heavy and rounded, dorsal fin originates just above or behind pectoral fins

Similar Species: Common Carp (pg. 72)

Goldfish	Common Carp	Goldfish	Common Carp
no chin barbels	chin barbels	dorsal fin originates just above or behind pectoral fins	dorsal fin originates just ahead of pectoral fins

GOLDFISH

Carassius auratus

Other Names: golden carp, Indiana, Baltimore or Missouri minnow

Habitat: quiet well-vegetated stream pools, weedy lake edges

Range: native to Asia, introduced throughout the world, central U.S. from coast to coast; in Illinois, few populations established throughout the state, common in the Illinois River

Food: scavengers on both plant and animal matter

Reproduction: long spawning season from late spring through summer; spawns in very shallow water at stream and lake edges; very sticky eggs are spread over vegetation; no parental care

Average Size: 3 to 10 inches

Records: State—none; North American—3 pounds, 2 ounces, Lourdes Pond, Indiana, 2002

Notes: This exotic fish has become established since the release of goldfish as pets or baitfish. Goldfish can become very common locally and are the predominant fish in some pools of the upper Illinois River where it passes through Chicago. Goldfish frequently hybridize with Common Carp and through a unique fertilization process sometimes form all-female populations. The brightly colored fish are very susceptible to predation, thus established populations are predominately olive green in color.

Description: dark green back; silver sides with a cross-hatched pattern; upturned mouth; eyes far forward and low on head; tiny trout-like scales; no scales on head

Similar Species: Bighead Carp (pg. 70), Common Carp (pg. 72), Grass Carp (pg. 74)

Silver Carp

keeled belly from gills to anal fin

Bighead Carp

keeled belly from pelvic fin to anal fin

Common Carp

large body scales

Grass Carp

scales showing prominent dark edge

Silver Carp

mouth lacks barbels

Common Carp

downturned sucker mouth with barbels, eyes high up

SILVER CARP
Hypophthalmichthys molitrix

Other Names: shiner carp

Habitat: quiet waters of large, warm rivers and connected lakes and ponds

Range: Asia, introduced in other parts of the world; in Illinois, Mississippi and Ohio Rivers and larger tributaries, lakes in the river flood plain

Food: aquatic vegetation, some floating algae

Reproduction: spawns from late spring to early summer in backwaters of large to midsized streams

Average Size: 24 to 36 inches, 5 to 50 pounds

Records: none

Notes: Silver Carp were introduced to Arkansas in the early '70s to control algae in aquaculture ponds and sewage lagoons, then escaped to the Mississippi River. Breeding populations are well established in the Ohio River and adjoining lakes. Combined with Bighead Carp, they are the predominant fish in some areas and have a very negative effect on river ecology. The Silver Carp, and to a lesser degree the Bighead Carp, makes high leaps from the water when frightened by boats. As algae feeders, they are targets for bow fishermen, but not anglers. They have limited food value in this country.

Description: dark olive back; silver-gray sides that reflect purple; large mouth; dark spot at base of dorsal fin; small barbel that fits in a groove between the back of the upper jaw and snout (very evident when the mouth is open)

Similar Species: Fathead Minnow (pg. 84)

Creek Chub

mouth extends to eye

Fathead Minnow

mouth does not extend to eye

CREEK CHUB

Semotilus atromaculatus

Cyprinidae

Other Names: common, brook, silver, mud or blackspot chub, horned or northern horned dace

Habitat: primarily found in quiet pools in clear streams and rivers, occasionally in lakes

Range: Montana southeast through the Gulf States; in Illinois, common throughout state except the Lake Michigan drainage

Food: small aquatic invertebrates and crustaceans

Reproduction: in late spring, male excavates a 1- to 3-foot long, teardrop-shaped pit at the head of stream riffles; using its mouth or rolling stones with its head, male fills pit to 6 to 8 inches high; females lay eggs on the mound, which are then covered and defended by the male; several other species spawn on the mounds, occasionally resulting in hybridization

Average Size: 4 to 10 inches, up to 8 ounces

Records: none

Notes: The Creek Chub is one of the most common stream fishes in eastern North America. They take bait readily and are often fished for by children spending a day on the creek. When water levels are low in late summer, the chub spawning mounds can be plentiful and quite evident leaving many to speculate on their origin. Chubs are a highly prized bait minnow, and local populations can be easily depleted by overharvesting.

81

Description: dark green, blotchy back; sides with two broad
lateral bands on a tan background; creamy red between
stripes; yellow belly; in breeding males, the belly turns
bright red; in females, the belly turns yellow-orange but
never red; very small scales

Similar Species: Fathead Minnow (pg. 84)

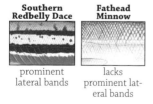

Southern Redbelly Dace	Fathead Minnow
prominent lateral bands	lacks prominent lateral bands

SOUTHERN REDBELLY DACE

Cyprinidae

Phoxinus erythrogaster

Other Names: redbelly or yellow-belly dace, leatherback

Habitat: small, clear streams with wooded and undercut banks

Range: north central U.S. with outlying populations in the Ozark Mountain Range; in Illinois, the northern third of the state

Food: bottom feeders on algae and plant matter

Reproduction: in early summer, a single female attended by several males spawns near the bottom in slow-moving pools; eggs hatch in 8 to 10 days without parental care

Average Size: 2 to 3 inches

Records: none

Notes: A small group of minnows in Illinois are referred to as daces. These small fish are primarily stream dwellers. The brightly colored Southern Redbelly Dace is one of Illinois's most beautiful fish and well-suited to be an aquarium fish. If the light is controlled, they will maintain their breeding colors for several months. Dace congregate in tightly packed schools when water levels are low, making them very susceptible to predators and overharvesting for bait.

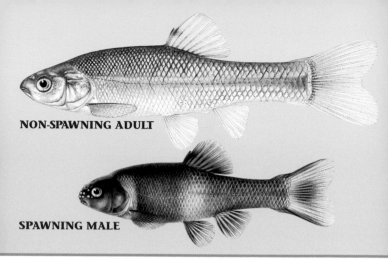

NON-SPAWNING ADULT

SPAWNING MALE

Description: olive to slate-gray back; dull golden yellow sides; dark side stripe narrows toward tail then widens to a dark spot; rounded snout and fins; no scales on head; dark blotch on front of dorsal fin

Similar Species: Creek Chub (pg. 80)

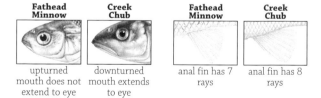

Fathead Minnow	Creek Chub	Fathead Minnow	Creek Chub
upturned mouth does not extend to eye	downturned mouth extends to eye	anal fin has 7 rays	anal fin has 8 rays

FATHEAD MINNOW

Pemephales promelas

Other Names: fathead, blackhead minnow, tuffy

Habitat: shallow pools of streams, shallow, weedy lakes and ponds

Range: east of the Rocky Mountains in the United States and Canada; in Illinois, common in the northeast 2/3 of the state, sporadic in southeast

Food: primarily plant matter, some insects and copepods (a variety of crustacean)

Reproduction: male prepares a nest beneath rocks and sticks; female enters and turns upside down to lay adhesive eggs on the overhang; the male fans the eggs and massages them with a special mucus-like pad on his back

Average Size: 3 to 4 inches

Records: none

Notes: There are over 1500 known minnow species in the world, 200 species of minnows found in North America, and 50 in Illinois. Carp and goldfish are minnows that were introduced from Asia, whereas native minnows are small fish, and are only a few inches to a foot long. The fathead minnow is one of Illinois' most numerous and widespread fish, and like the Bluntnose Minnow, is a common bait minnow. These minnows are certainly two of the most economically important fish in the U.S.

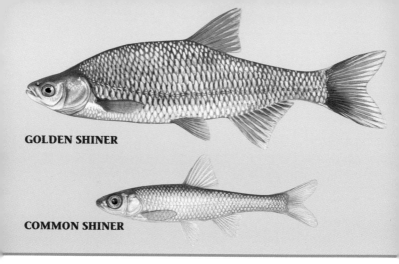

GOLDEN SHINER

COMMON SHINER

Description: back gold to greenish-gold; sides golden with silver reflections; belly is yellowish-silver; deep slab-sided body; mouth angled up; long triangle-shaped head

Similar Species: Common Shiner, Creek Chub (pg. 80)

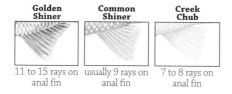

Golden Shiner	Common Shiner	Creek Chub
11 to 15 rays on anal fin	usually 9 rays on anal fin	7 to 8 rays on anal fin

GOLDEN SHINER
Notemigonus crysoleucas

Other Names: bream, American bream, roach, American roach, butterfish, pond shiner

Habitat: clear, weedy ponds and quiet streams

Range: native to eastern U.S. south to Florida, introduced in the West; in Illinois, common throughout the state

Food: plankton, crustaceans, aquatic insects, mollusks

Reproduction: extended midsummer spawning season; a female attended by one or two males spreads adhesive eggs over submerged vegetation; no parental care

Average Size: 3 to 7 inches

Records: none

Notes: There are almost twenty Illinois minnows called shiners and most are in the genus *Notropis*. The Golden Shiner is a large showy minnow that congregates in large schools, particularly when young. Not all shiners are as flashy as the name indicates; some are dull and show almost no silver on the sides. Sometimes found in open water, but never far from vegetation, Golden Shiners are an important forage and baitfish. Common Shiners are native to the rocky streams of northern Illinois and are now widely propagated and sold for bait. In many areas, Common Shiners have replaced Golden Shiners as the preferred bait shiner.

Description: dark green to dark blue back and upper sides; bright silver or golden sides; large yellow-tinged eye; large scales; thin body flattened from side to side with a sharp scale ridge (keel) from throat to pelvic fin; forward-facing mouth with small teeth

Similar Species: Gizzard Shad (pg. 60), Mooneye (pg. 90), Skipjack Herring (pg. 58)

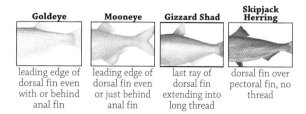

Goldeye	**Mooneye**	**Gizzard Shad**	**Skipjack Herring**
leading edge of dorsal fin even with or behind anal fin	leading edge of dorsal fin even or just behind anal fin	last ray of dorsal fin extending into long thread	dorsal fin over pectoral fin, no thread

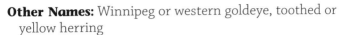

GOLDEYE
Hiodon alosoides

Hiodontidae

Other Names: Winnipeg or western goldeye, toothed or yellow herring

Habitat: large lakes and quiet backwaters of large, turbid (cloudy) streams and rivers

Range: Hudson Bay drainage south through the Ohio and Mississippi drainage to Tennessee; in Illinois, common in the Mississippi and Illinois Rivers, less common in the Ohio and Wabash Rivers, sporadic in rest of state

Food: insects, small fish, crayfish, snails

Reproduction: spawning takes place in turbid pools and backwaters when water temperatures reach the mid-50s

Average Size: 12 to 18 inches, 1 to 2 pounds

Records: State—2 pounds, 1 ounce, Embarras River, Cumberland County, 1998; North American—3 pounds, 13 ounces, Ohae Tailwater, South Dakota, 1987

Notes: The Goldeye's large yellow eye is an adaptation for low-light conditions and enables it to feed at night and navigate dark, silty waters. They feed near the surface in quiet pools, and are associated with Mooneyes. Harvested commercially from large Canadian lakes for 150 years, they were supposedly served on the Canadian Pacific Railway as Winnipeg smoked Goldeye. While not often an angler's target, Goldeyes readily take flies and small lures and are frequently caught while fishing for other species. They are still fairly common in the Mississippi River near the mouth of the Missouri River.

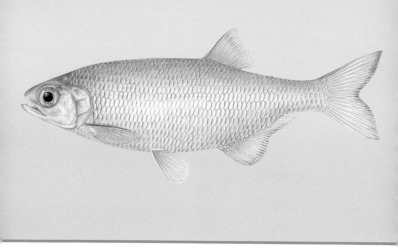

Description: olive back; silver sides; large scales on the body, none on the head; large white eye is over 1/3 the width of the head; thin body flattened with a sharp, scaleless keel between the pelvic and anal fins; terminal mouth

Similar Species: Gizzard Shad (pg. 60), Goldeye (pg. 88), Skipjack Herring (pg. 58)

Mooneye	**Gizzard Shad**	**Goldeye**	**Skipjack Herring**
front edge of dorsal even or behind anal fin	last ray of dorsal extends into a thread	leading edge of dorsal even or behind anal fin	dorsal fin over pectoral fin, no thread

Mooneye	**Gizzard Shad**
lower jaw protrudes beyond snout	snout protruding over mouth

MOONEYE
Hiodon tergisus

Other Names: white shad, slicker, toothed herring, river whitefish

Habitat: clear, quiet waters of large lakes and the backwaters of large streams

Range: Hudson Bay drainage east to the St. Lawrence, through the Mississippi drainage south into Arkansas and Alabama; in Illinois, the Mississippi and Illinois Rivers, rare in the Ohio and Wabash drainages

Food: insects, small fish, crayfish, snails

Reproduction: adults migrate up larger tributaries to spawn in early spring when water temperatures reach the mid-50s; gelatin-coated eggs are released over gravel bars in fast currents

Average Size: 12 inches, 12 ounces to 1 pound

Records: State—none; North American—1 pound, 1 ounce, Lake Poygan, Wisconsin, 2000

Notes: Mooneyes are small, flashy fish that jump repeatedly when hooked, and commonly feed on insects in slack waters of large lakes and rivers. However, they are bony with little meat, except along the back, and are not good table fare. Once commercially harvested in some states, Mooneyes are declining over much of their range, and Illinois is no exception. Though small, they are related to Arapaima, the world's largest scaled freshwater fish.

Description: olive green back; tan to yellow-brown sides with faint, wavy vertical bars; rounded tail; dark bar just before the tail; slightly flattened head

Similar Species: Fathead Minnow (pg. 84), Mosquitofish (pg. 68)

Central Mudminnow

rounded tail

Fathead Minnow

forked tail

Central Mudminnow

mouth not upturned, no bar under eye

Mosquitofish

terminal mouth, bar under eye

CENTRAL MUDMINNOW

Umbridae

Umbra limi

Other Names: Mississippi or western mudminnow, dogfish, mudfish

Habitat: slow, stagnant waters of weedy streams and ponds with soft bottoms

Range: Great Lake states through the Midwest; in Illinois, common in the north, rare or extirpated in the southeast

Food: insects, mollusks, larger crustaceans

Reproduction: in the early spring, adults move into flooded pools when water temperatures reach the mid-50s; yellow-orange eggs are deposited singly on plant leaves and are left to hatch without parental care

Average Size: 2 to 4 inches

Records: none

Notes: This hardy little fish can withstand very low oxygen levels and can gulp air to breathe (even from air bubbles under the ice). They are frequently the only fish left in ponds after winter die-offs. They hide in the bottom detritus but do not bury themselves tail-first in the mud, as often reported. They are a good baitfish, withstanding the bait pail and hooks well. They can be fun aquarium fish and quickly learn to eat small pieces of meat or angleworms when offered.

Description: large, gray, scaleless body; snout protrudes into a large paddle; shark-like forked tail; gills extend into long, pointed flaps

Similar Species: none

PADDLEFISH

Polyodon spathula

Other Names: spoonbill cat, duckbill

Habitat: deep pools of large rivers and their connecting lakes

Range: large rivers in the Mississippi drainage; in Illinois, once common in the Mississippi, Illinois, Ohio, Wabash Rivers and larger tributaries, now rare

Food: free-swimming plankton

Reproduction: spawning takes place when water levels are rising in the spring and temperatures reach the low 50s; adults migrate up large tributaries until blocked by dams; breeding schools gather in moving water less than 10 feet deep to release eggs over large gravel bars

Average Size: 2 to 4 feet, 20 to 40 pounds

Records: State—none; North American—144 pounds, Dam #7, Kansas, 2004

Notes: This prehistoric fish is very shark-like in anatomy, with its only close relative found in the Yangtze River of China. Paddlefish have a large mouth but no teeth and feed entirely on plankton. The function of the paddle is not well understood, but it is not used to dig in the mud as once suspected. Scientists believe that sensors in the paddle detect electrical currents created by clouds of plankton. The constructions of locks and dams have greatly reduced the Paddlefish population in most of the state. Once an important commercial fish in Illinois for both meat and caviar, it is now reduced to sport fishing levels.

Description: tan to olive back and upper sides with dark blotches and speckles; sides tan to golden with X, Y and W patterns; breeding males dark with black bars

Similar Species: Logperch (pg. 104)

Johnny Darter

dorsal fins obviously separated

Logperch

dorsal fins slightly separated

JOHNNY DARTER

Etheostoma nigrum

Other Names: red-sided, yellowbelly or weed darter

Habitat: lakes that have some vegetation or algae mat; clear, slow-flowing streams

Range: Rocky Mountains east across Canada and the U.S. through the Great Lakes region; in Illinois, common through-out the state except in southern and west-central streams

Food: small aquatic invertebrates

Reproduction: in May and June, males migrate to shorelines to establish breeding areas; females move from territory to territory, spawning with several males; each sequence produces 7 to 10 eggs which sink and attach to the bottom

Average Size: 2 to 4 inches

Records: none

Notes: Relatives of the Yellow Perch and Walleye, darters are primarily stream fish well-adapted to living among rocks in fast current. A small swim bladder allows darters to sink rapidly to the bottom after a "dart" and thereby avoid being swept away by the current. Darters are hard to see when they move, but are easy to spot when perched on their pectoral fins. Johnny Darters prefer weedy lake shorelines but can be found in a wide range of habitats.

Description: slender body; gray, dark silver or brown with dark side blotches; black spots on spiny dorsal; some white on lower tail margin; lacks Walleye's white tail spot

Similar Species: Saugeye (pg. 100), Walleye (pg. 102)

Sauger	**Saugeye**	**Walleye**
dorsal has distinct circular spots, no spot on rear base	dorsal has distinct spots and blotch at rear base	dorsal fin has indistinct spots, dark blotch on rear base

Sauger	**Saugeye**	**Walleye**
cheeks rough and few scales	cheeks rough with scales	cheeks smooth and few scales

SAUGER

Sander canadensis

Other Names: sand, spotfin or river pike, jackfish, jack salmon

Habitat: large lakes and rivers

Range: large lakes in southern Canada, the northern U.S. and the wider reaches of the Mississippi, Missouri, Ohio and Tennessee River drainages; in Illinois, common in the Mississippi River, sporadic in other large rivers and Lake Michigan

Food: small fish, aquatic insects, crayfish

Reproduction: spawns in April and May as water approaches 50 degrees; adults move into the shallow waters of tributaries and headwaters to randomly deposit eggs over gravel beds

Average Size: 10 to 12 inches, 8 ounces to 2 pounds

Records: State—5 pounds, 13 ounces, Mississippi River, Jo Daviess County, 1967; North American—8 pounds, 12 ounces, Lake Sakakawea, North Dakota, 1971

Notes: Though the Sauger is the Walleye's smaller cousin, it is a big-water fish primarily found in large lakes and rivers. It is slow-growing and often reaches only two pounds in twenty years. The Sauger populations in the Mississippi River are still strong, but they have been greatly reduced in the Illinois, Ohio and Wabash rivers and there are no recent records in the upper Illinois. Saugers are aggressive daytime feeders compared to Walleye. Their fine, flavored flesh is top table fare.

Description: slender body; gray, dark silver or brown with dark side blotches; two dorsals, front spiny, rear has soft rays; dark spots on spiny dorsal; lacks Walleye's white tail spot

Similar Species: Sauger (pg. 98), Walleye (pg. 102)

Saugeye	Sauger	Walleye
dorsal has distinct spots and blotch at rear base	dorsal has distinct circular spots, no spot on rear base	dorsal fin has indistinct spots, dark blotch on rear base
cheeks rough with scales	cheeks rough and few scales	cheeks smooth and few scales

SAUGEYE

Sander vitreus x Sander canadensis

Other Names: saugie, rivereye

Habitat: stocked in lakes, reservoirs and streams; may become established below dams

Range: hatchery-produced fish stocked in midwestern and western states; in Illinois, commonly stocked in lakes and rivers, well-established below some dam spillways

Food: mainly small fish, but also eats insects, crayfish

Reproduction: spawning behavior similar to Walleye and Sauger

Average Size: 13 to 16 inches, 1 to 2 pounds

Records: State—9 pounds, 11 ounces, Evergreen Lake, McLean County, 2001; North American—15 pounds, 10 ounces, Fort Peck Reservoir, Montana, 1995

Notes: Saugeyes are produced in hatcheries using Walleye eggs and Sauger sperm. In terms of appearance and behavior they share characteristics with both Walleyes and Saugers. They tolerate warm water and turbidity better than Walleyes and are well-adapted to both lakes and streams. On average they are bigger than Saugers, but smaller than Walleyes. Unlike many other hybrids, they are fertile and can breed with both Walleyes and Saugers, producing fish with many genetic problems. Saugeyes are increasingly being stocked in waters unsuitable for Walleyes.

Description: long, round body; dark silver or golden to dark olive brown in color; spines in both first dorsal and anal fin; sharp canine teeth; dark spot at base of the three last spines of the dorsal fin; white spot on bottom lobe of tail

Similar Species: Sauger (pg. 98), Saugeye (pg. 100)

Walleye	**Sauger**	**Saugeye**
spiny dorsal with indistinct spots, dark blotch on rear base	spiny dorsal with distinct spots, no blotch on rear base	spiny dorsal fin with distinct spots, dark blotch on rear base
Walleye	**Sauger**	**Saugeye**
white spot on bottom lobe of tail	no white spot on tail	no white spot on bottom of tail

WALLEYE

Sander vitreus

Other Names: marble-eyes, walleyed pike, jack, jackfish, Susquehanna salmon

Habitat: lakes and streams, abundant in very large lakes

Range: originally the northern states and Canada, now widely stocked throughout the U.S.; in Illinois, common in the Mississippi and Rock Rivers but sporadic in other rivers; stocked in reservoirs, uncommon to rare in Illinois waters of Lake Michigan

Food: mainly small fish, but also eats insects, crayfish, and leeches

Reproduction: spawns in tributary streams or rocky lake shoals when spring water temperatures reach 45–50 degrees; no parental care

Average Size: 14 to 17 inches, 1 to 3 pounds

Records: State—14 pounds, Kankakee River, Kankakee County, 1961; North American—21 pounds, 11 ounces, Greer's Ferry Lake, Arkansas, 1982

Notes: Revered by anglers, and one of the most popular sport fish. Not a strong fighter, but fine table fare. A reflective layer of pigment in the eye allows it to see in low-light conditions. As a result, Walleyes are most active at dusk, dawn and throughout the night and during other light-reduced conditions such as overcast skies and beneath waves sometimes called "Walleye chop." Native to Illinois' rivers and floodplain lakes, Walleyes are now stocked throughout the state.

103

Description: back yellowish-brown to olive; sides lighter with 15 to 25 dark vertical bands; prominent dark spot at base of tail; pointed snout; long cylindrical body

Similar Species: Johnny Darter (pg. 96)

Logperch	**Johnny Darter**
larger mouth overhung by conical snout	small mouth, blunt nose

Logperch	**Johnny Darter**
dorsal fins slightly separated	dorsal fins obviously separated

Logperch	**Johnny Darter**
sides with W, X, and Y marks	side with dark, vertical bands

LOGPERCH

Percina carprodes

Percidae

Other Names: log or Manitou Darter, zebra fish, rockfish

Habitat: medium to large streams and rivers and large lakes

Range: Saskatchewan and Quebec, through the Great Lake states into the central U.S. to the Gulf; in Illinois, common throughout the state, particularly in the Illinois River

Food: small aquatic invertebrates and algae

Reproduction: in late spring adults move to the shallows; males form small mating schools (10 to 15 fish) that hover around a single female; adhesive eggs are deposited at random on sand; no parental care

Average Size: 3 to 6 inches

Records: none

Notes: The Logperch is the largest of the darters and is sometimes caught by anglers fishing for perch. When caught, they are frequently mistaken for small perch or walleye. Logperch are a common forage for game fish but are not hardy enough to be a good baitfish. However, they are showy and active and make good aquarium fish.

Description: 6 to 9 olive-green vertical bars on a yellow-brown background; two separate dorsal fins—the front fin consists entirely of spines, the back fins consist of soft rays; the lower fins are tinged yellow or orange and brighter in breeding males

Similar Species: Logperch (pg. 104), Walleye (pg. 102)

Yellow Perch	Logperch	Yellow Perch	Walleye
dorsal fins obviously separated	dorsal fins slightly separated	lacks prominent white spot on tail	white spot on bottom of tail

YELLOW PERCH

Perca flavescens

Other Names: ringed, striped, or jack perch

Habitat: lakes and streams, prefers clear, open water

Range: widely introduced throughout southern Canada and the northern U.S.; in Illinois, common throughout the state including Lake Michigan

Food: minnows, insects, snails, leeches, and crayfish

Reproduction: spawns at night in shallow, weedy areas when water temperatures reach 45 degrees; females drape gelatinous ribbons of eggs over submerged vegetation

Average Size: 8 to 11 inches, 6 to 10 ounces

Records: State—2 pounds, 9 ounces, Arrowhead Club Lake, Will County, 1974; North American—4 pounds, 3 ounces, Bordentown, New Jersey, 1865

Notes: Yellow Perch are very common in Lake Michigan and are possibly the most important food and sport fish in the lake. Perch congregate in large schools and are active throughout the year, providing endless hours of enjoyment for anglers. Yellow perch reproduction in the Great Lakes seems to be adversely affected by high Alewife populations. The perch population quickly recovers in years that the Alewife population crashes. Due to increased turbidity, perch are becoming extremely rare in some waters where they once flourished, including the upper Illinois River.

Description: olive green to yellow-brown back and sides; wavy yellowish bars on sides; dark teardrop below eye; fins cream to pale yellow; scales on entire cheek and gill covers

Similar Species: Northern Pike (pg. 112)

Grass Pickerel / Northern Pike

scales on entire gill cover

lower half of gill cover unscaled

Grass Pickerel

vertical bar under eye, forehead concave

Northern Pike

no vertical bar under eye, forehead convex

GRASS PICKEREL

Esocidae

Esox americanus vermiculatus

Common Names: mud or little pickerel, grass or mud pike

Habitat: shallow, weedy lakes and sluggish streams

Range: eastern one-third of the United States from the Great Lakes basin to Maine and south to Florida and west through the Gulf states; in Illinois, common in the eastern half of the state, sporadic in the west

Food: small fish, aquatic insects

Reproduction: spawns in early spring just as the ice goes out; adults enter flooded meadows and shallow bays to lay eggs in less than 2 feet of water; adhesive eggs are deposited over shallow, submerged vegetation; no parental care

Size: 10 to 12 inches, under 1 pound

Records: State—none; North American—1 pound, Dewart Lake, Indiana, 1990

Notes: The Grass Pickerel is the smallest Illinois member of the pike family and inhabits the dense vegetation in slow-moving streams and smaller lakes. In large lakes they congregate near stream mouths. Pickerel readily take small lures and minnows and are often caught by anglers that think they are baby pike. At times they can be a nuisance for panfish anglers. It is unclear what relationship there is between the Grass Pickerel and the Northern Pike. In some lakes they coexist, while in others there is just one species or the other.

MUSKELLUNGE

TIGER MUSKIE

Description: torpedo-shaped body; dorsal fin near tail; dark gray-green back; silver to silver-green sides; dark vertical bars or blotches on sides (dark markings on light background); tail lobes pointed

Similar Species: Grass Pickerel (pg. 108), Northern Pike (pg. 112), Tiger Muskie (pg. 110)

Muskellunge	**Northern Pike**
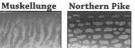	
dark marks on light background	light marks on dark background

Muskellunge	**Northern Pike**
6 or more pores on each side under the jaw	5 or fewer pores on each side under the jaw

Muskellunge	**Grass Pickerel**	**Northern Pike**	**Tiger Muskie**
pointed tail	rounded tail	rounded tail	rounded tail

MUSKELLUNGE

Esox masquinongy

Other Names: muskie, Great Lakes or Ohio Muskellunge

Habitat: waters of large, clear, weedy lakes; medium to large rivers with slow currents and deep pools

Range: the Great Lakes basin east to Maine, south through the Ohio River drainage to Tennessee; in Illinois, native to Lake Michigan; Muskies or Tiger Muskies are now stocked in some lakes and streams

Food: small fish

Reproduction: spawning takes place in late spring when the water temperature reaches 50 to 60 degrees; eggs are laid in dead vegetation in tributary streams or shallow bays

Average Size: 30 to 42 inches, 10 to 20 pounds

Records: State—38 pounds, 8 ounces, Kaskaskia River, Shelby County, 2002; North American—69 pounds, 11 ounces, Chippewa Flowage, Wisconsin, 1949

Notes: The Muskellunge is the prize of all fresh water game fishing. This large, fast predator prefers large, shallow, clear lakes. Muskies are uncommon to rare over most of their range, and in Illinois were probably only native in Lake Michigan. They are hard to entice with lures or bait, and muskie fishermen average over 50 hours to catch a legal fish. Muskellunge readily hybridize with Northern Pike (Tiger Muskellunge) and pure muskie stock is rare. Tiger Muskellunge are now reared and stocked in some of Illinois' larger lakes.

Description: dark green back; light green sides with bean-shaped light spots on a dark background; elongated body with a dorsal fin near the tail; head is long and flattened in front, forming a duck-like snout

Similar Species: Grass Pickerel (pg. 108), Muskellunge (pg. 110), Tiger Muskie (pg. 110)

Northern Pike	**Muskellunge**
rounded tail	pointed tail

Northern Pike	**Muskellunge**
5 or fewer pores on under-side of jaw	6 or more pores on each side under the jaw

Northern Pike	**Muskellunge**	**Tiger Muskie**
light spots on dark background	dark marks on light background	dark marks on light background

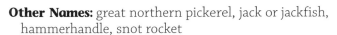

NORTHERN PIKE

Esox lucius

Esocidae

Other Names: great northern pickerel, jack or jackfish, hammerhandle, snot rocket

Habitat: lakes and slow-moving streams, often associated with vegetation

Range: northern Europe, Asia, and North America; in Illinois, common in the northern third of the state and Lake Michigan

Food: small fish, occasionally frogs, crayfish

Reproduction: in early spring as water temperatures reach 34 to 40 degrees, eggs are laid among shallow vegetation in tributary streams or lake edges; no parental care

Average Size: 18 to 24 inches, 2 to 5 pounds

Records: State—26 pounds, 15 ounces, Strip Mine Lake, Kankakee County, 1989; North American—46 pounds, 2 ounces, Great Sacandaga Lake, New York, 1940

Notes: This large, fast predator is one of the most wide-spread freshwater fish in the world and a prime sport fish throughout its range. Its long, tube-shaped body and intra-muscular bones are adaptations for quick bursts of speed. Pike are sight feeders and hunt by lying in wait and capture their prey with a lightning-fast lunge. Many anglers have lost their catch near the boat when the pike employed this burst of speed to escape. The Tiger Muskellunge is a hybrid of the Northern Pike and the Muskellunge.

113

Description: back is olive, blue-gray to black with worm-like markings; sides bronze to olive with red spots tinged light brown; lower fins are red-orange with a white leading edge; tail squared or slightly forked

Similar Species: Brown Trout (pg. 116), Lake Trout (pg. 118), Rainbow Trout (pg. 120), Splake (pg. 118)

Brook Trout	Brown Trout	Lake Trout	Rainbow Trout
worm-like markings, with red center spots	large, dark spots, small red dots	sides lack red spots	pink stripe on silver body

Brook Trout	Lake Trout	Splake
tail square to slightly forked	tail deeply forked	tail moderately forked

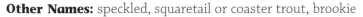

BROOK TROUT

Salvelinus fontinalis

Salmonidae

Other Names: speckled, squaretail or coaster trout, brookie

Habitat: cool, clear streams and small lakes with sand/gravel bottoms and moderate vegetation; coastal waters of Great Lakes near tributaries

Range: Great Lakes region north to Labrador, south through the Appalachians to Georgia, introduced into the western U.S., Canada, Europe, and South America; in Illinois, Lake Michigan and a few clear streams

Food: insects, small fish

Reproduction: spawns in late fall when temperatures reach 40 to 49 degrees; also spawns in lakes where springs can aerate eggs; female builds 4- to 12-inch-deep nest, then buries fertilized eggs in loose gravel; eggs hatch in 50 to 150 days

Average Size: 8 to 10 inches, 8 ounces

Records: State—7 pounds, 5 ounces, Lake Michigan, Lake County, 1998; North American—14 pounds, 8 ounces, Nipigon River, Ontario, 1916

Notes: The Brook Trout is a beautiful fish native to Illinois only in Lake Michigan. The Brook Trout population crashed due to the introduction of the Alewife, but the population has rebounded with persistent stocking. Brook Trout require cool, clean water and are stocked in only a few suitable Illinois streams. There is little or no natural trout reproduction in such streams. The bright, orange flesh of Brook Trout is firm and has a delicate flavor prized by trout fishermen.

115

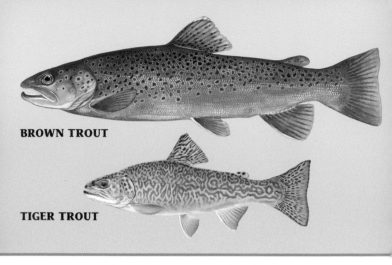

BROWN TROUT

TIGER TROUT

Description: golden brown to dark olive back and sides; creamy white to orange belly; spots on sides, dorsal fin and sometimes upper lobe of tail; few red spots with light halos

Similar Species: Brook Trout (pg. 114), Lake Trout (pg. 118), Rainbow Trout (pg. 120), Tiger Trout (pg. 116)

Brown Trout	**Lake Trout**	**Rainbow Trout**
dark spots on brown or olive	white spots on dark background	pink stripe on silvery body

Brown Trout	**Brook Trout**	**Tiger Trout**
lacks worm-like markings on back and sides	worm-like markings on back	worm-like markings on back and sides

116

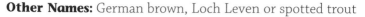

BROWN TROUT
Salmo trutta

Other Names: German brown, Loch Leven or spotted trout

Habitat: open ocean near spawning streams and clear, cold, gravel-bottomed streams; shallow portions of the Great Lakes

Range: native to Europe from the Mediterranean to Arctic Norway and Siberia, introduced worldwide; in Illinois, stocked in Lake Michigan and reported in a few northern streams

Food: insects, crayfish, small fish

Reproduction: spawns October-December in headwater streams, tributaries and stream mouths when migration is blocked; female fans out saucer-shaped nest that male guards until spawning; female covers eggs

Average Size: 11 to 20 inches, 2 to 6 pounds

Records: State—36 pounds, 11.5 ounces, Lake Michigan, Cook County, 1997; North American—40 pounds, 4 ounces, Little Red River, Arkansas, 1992

Notes: This European trout was brought to North America in the late 1800s where it soon replaced the Brook Trout in many streams. Brown Trout prefer cold, clear streams but will tolerate much warmer water. Fish stocked in Lake Michigan do well. Prized by fly-fisherman the world over, this trout is a secretive, hard-to-catch fish that has a fine, delicate flavor. Brown Trout often aggressively feed on cloudy, rainy days and at night. Brown Trout hybridize with Brook Trout to produce the colorful but sterile Tiger Trout.

117

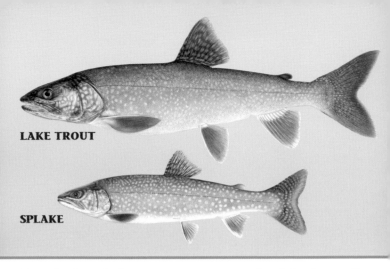

LAKE TROUT

SPLAKE

Description: dark gray to gray-green on head, back, top fins and tail; white spots on the sides and unpaired fins (light spots on dark background); tail deeply forked; inside of mouth is white

Similar Species: Brook Trout (pg. 114), Splake

Lake Trout

tail deeply forked

Brook Trout

tail square to slightly forked

Splake

tail moderately forked

Lake Trout

lacks worm-like markings

Brook Trout

worm-like marks on back

118

LAKE TROUT
Salvelinus namaycush

Other Names: togue, mackinaw, great gray trout, laker

Habitat: oxygen-rich waters of deep, clear, infertile lakes with water colder than 65 degrees

Range: Great Lakes north through Canada, the northeastern United States, stocked in the Rocky Mountains; in Illinois, native to Lake Michigan

Food: small fish, insects

Reproduction: females scatter eggs over rocky lake shoals when water temperatures dip below 50 degrees in fall

Average Size: 15 to 20 inches, 7 to 10 pounds

Records: State—38 pounds, 4 ounces, Lake Michigan, Lake County, 1999; North American—74 pounds, 2 ounces, Great Bear Lake, N.W.T., Canada, 1995

Notes: Although the Lake Trout is native to Illinois, it is more common in cool, northern sections of Lake Michigan. Once an important part of the Lake Michigan fishery and a prized food and sport fish, Lake Trout populations were decimated in the early 1950s by overfishing and the introduction of the Sea Lamprey. Thanks to restocking efforts and aggressive lamprey control, the population has returned to sport fishing levels. Lake Trout are caught by trolling deep in summer or "surf" fishing in shallower water during the spring and fall.

Description: blue-green to brown head and back; silver lower sides with pink to rose stripes; entire body covered with small black spots; adipose fin

Similar Species: Brook Trout (pg. 114), Brown Trout (pg. 116), Pink Salmon (pg. 126)

Rainbow Trout lacks worm-like markings	**Brook Trout** worm-like marks on back	**Rainbow Trout** pinkish stripe on silvery body

Brown Trout sides lack pinkish stripe	

Rainbow Trout white mouth	**Pink Salmon** dark tongue and jaw tip

RAINBOW TROUT
Oncorhynchus mykiss

Salmonidae

Other Names: steelhead, Pacific, Kamloops or silver trout

Habitat: prefers whitewater in cool streams and coastal regions of large lakes; tolerates smaller, cool, clear lakes

Range: Pacific Ocean and coastal streams from Mexico to Alaska and northeastern Russia, introduced worldwide including in the Great Lakes and eastern U.S.; stocked in Lake Michigan and other lakes and streams in Illinois

Food: insects, small crustaceans, fish

Reproduction: predominantly spring spawners but some fall spawning varieties exist; female builds nest in well-aerated gravel in both streams and lakes

Average Size: streams—10 to 12 inches, 1 pound; lakes—20 to 22 inches, 2 to 3 pounds

Records: State—31 pounds, 6.7 ounces, Lake Michigan, Lake County, 1993; North American—42 pounds, 2 ounces, Bell Island, Alaska, 1970

Notes: The first attempts to stock this Pacific trout in Illinois were made in the late 1800s and stocking efforts have continued to the present day, with varying degrees of success. Introducing Steelheads into Lake Michigan has created an exciting sport fishery there, though there are no continually reproducing stream populations in Illinois; the Rainbow Trout caught in Illinois today are the result of continuous restocking. Rainbow Trout that migrate from spawning streams into the open ocean for part of their life are called Steelheads.

121

Description: iridescent green to blue-green back and upper sides; silver below the lateral line; small black spots on the back and tail; inside of the mouth is dark; breeding males are olive brown to purple with pronounced kype (hooked snout)

Similar Species: Coho Salmon (pg. 124), Pink Salmon (pg. 126), Rainbow Trout (pg. 120)

Chinook Salmon	**Coho Salmon**	**Pink Salmon**
small spots throughout tail	spots only in top half of tail	eye-sized spots throughout tail

Chinook Salmon	**Coho Salmon**	**Rainbow Trout**
inside of mouth is dark	inside of mouth is gray	inside of mouth is white

122

CHINOOK SALMON

Oncorhynchus tshawytscha

Other Names: king or spring salmon, tyee, quinnat, black mouth

Habitat: open ocean and large, clear, gravel-bottomed rivers; open waters of the Great Lakes and spawning streams

Range: Pacific Ocean north from California to Japan, introduced to the Atlantic coast; in Illinois, Lake Michigan and mouths of larger tributary streams

Food: insects, small fish, crustaceans

Reproduction: matures in 3 to 5 years; in September and October they migrate up streams to spawn on gravel bars; eggs hatch the following spring; adults die shortly after spawning

Average Size: 24 to 30 inches, 15 to 20 pounds

Records: State—37 pounds, Lake Michigan, Lake County, 1976; North American—97 pounds, 4 ounces, Kenai River, Alaska 1985

Notes: The largest member of the salmon family, Chinooks may reach forty pounds in landlocked lakes and may be even larger in the Pacific. Prior to the 1960s, many unsuccessful attempts were made to introduce Chinook Salmon into the Great Lakes region. Since then, a stable population of hatchery-reared fish have been maintained in Lake Michigan, creating an important sport fishery. Though Chinooks enter streams in the fall in an attempt to spawn, there is little or no natural reproduction.

Description: dark metallic blue to green back; silver sides and belly; small dark spots on back, sides and upper half of tail; inside of mouth is gray; breeding adults have a gray to green head with red to maroon sides; males develop kype (hooked snout)

Similar Species: Chinook Salmon (pg. 122), Pink Salmon (pg. 126), Rainbow Trout (pg. 120)

Coho Salmon

spots only in top half of tail

Chinook Salmon

small spots throughout tail

Pink Salmon

eye-sized spots throughout tail

Coho Salmon

inside of mouth is gray

Rainbow Trout

inside of mouth is white

124

COHO SALMON

Oncorhynchus kisutch

Other Names: silver salmon, sea trout, blueback

Habitat: open ocean near spawning streams and clear, gravel-bottomed streams; open Great Lakes waters within 10 miles of shore

Range: Pacific Ocean north from California to Japan, the Atlantic coast of the U.S., the Great Lakes; in Illinois, Lake Michigan and mouths of larger tributary streams

Food: insects, smelt, alewives

Reproduction: spawns in October and November; adults migrate up streams to build nests on gravel bars; parent fish die shortly after spawning

Average Size: 20 inches, 4 to 5 pounds

Records: State—20 pounds, 9 ounces, Lake Michigan, Lake County, 1972; North American—33 pounds, 4 ounces, Salmon River, New York, 1989

Notes: This Pacific salmon was first stocked in Lake Michigan in 1967 and is now a well established sport fish. Coho Salmon migrate up streams to spawn in the fall after spending two years in the open lake, but they do not reproduce well in any of the Great Lakes and current populations are maintained by stocking. A very strong fighter and excellent table fare, they are one of the largest fish to be routinely caught in Illinois' waters. When mature, some Coho Salmon may reach twenty pounds or more.

Description: steel blue to blue-green back with silver sides; dark spots on back and tail, some as large as the eye; breeding males develop a large hump in front of the dorsal fin and a hooked upper jaw (kype); both sexes are pink during spawning

Similar Species: Brown Trout (pg. 116), Chinook Salmon (pg. 122), Coho Salmon (pg. 124), Rainbow Trout (pg. 120)

Pink Salmon	**Brown Trout**	**Coho Salmon**	**Rainbow Trout**
dark tongue and jaw tip	inside of mouth is white	inside of mouth is gray	inside of mouth is white

Pink Salmon	**Chinook Salmon**	**Coho Salmon**
eye-sized spots throughout tail	small spots throughout tail	spots only in top half of tail

PINK SALMON

Oncorhynchus gorbuscha

Other Names: autumn or humpback salmon, humpy

Habitat: coastal Pacific Ocean and open water of the Great Lakes, spawns in clear streams

Range: Coastal Pacific Ocean from northern California to Alaska, Great Lakes; in Illinois, Lake Michigan

Food: small fish, crustaceans

Reproduction: spawns in tributary streams usually at two years of age; female builds nests on gravel bars, then covers fertilized eggs; adults die after spawning

Average Size: 17 to 19 inches, 1 to 2 pounds

Records: State—3 pounds, 4 ounces, Lake Michigan, Lake County, 1992; North American—12 pounds, 9 ounces, Moose and Kenai Rivers, Alaska, 1974

Notes: This Pacific salmon was unintentionally released into Lake Superior's Thunder Bay in 1956 and has spread throughout the Great Lakes. Pink Salmon spend two to three years in the open lake then move into streams to spawn and die. Pink Salmon are infrequently seen in Illinois spawning streams, but a few are caught by anglers each year. They are not considered good table fare, as the flesh deteriorates rapidly and must quickly be put on ice.

Description: silver with faint pink or purple tinge; dark back; light-colored tail; small mouth; long body but deeper than Rainbow Smelt

Similar Species: Mooneye (pg. 90), Rainbow Smelt (pg. 134)

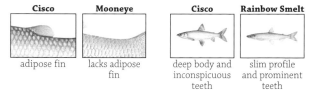

Cisco	**Mooneye**	**Cisco**	**Rainbow Smelt**
adipose fin	lacks adipose fin	deep body and inconspicuous teeth	slim profile and prominent teeth

CISCO

Coregonus artedi

Other Names: shallow water, common or Great Lakes cisco, lake herring, tullibee

Habitat: shoal waters of the Great Lakes and nutrient-poor inland lakes with oxygen-rich depths that remain cool during summer

Range: northeastern U.S., Great Lakes and Canada; in Illinois, Lake Michigan and rarely the Illinois River mouth

Food: plankton, small crustaceans, aquatic insects

Reproduction: spawns in November and December when water temperatures reach the lower 30s; eggs are deposited over clean bottoms, in 3 to 8 feet of water

Average Size: 10 to 12 inches, 1 pound

Records: State—none; North American—7 pounds, 4 ounces, Cedar Lake, Manitoba, 1986

Notes: Ciscoes were once the most productive commercial fish in the Great Lakes and occasionally migrated far up the Illinois River. The population collapsed due to overfishing, pollution, and the introduction of nonnative species. No longer of commercial importance, Ciscoes can still be caught through the ice in winter and by fly-fishermen in summer. Ciscoes vary in body structure and may appear torpedo-shaped or as deep-bodied fish. Ciscoes imported from Canada are often marketed as "smoked whitefish."

Description: slate-gray to blotchy olive-brown back; dark brown streaks on fins; large mouth; eyes set almost on top of the head; large, winglike pectoral fins; lacks scales

Similar Species: Round Goby (pg. 54)

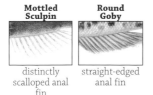

Mottled Sculpin	Round Goby
distinctly scalloped anal fin	straight-edged anal fin

Mottled Sculpin	Round Goby
lacks scales	scales present

MOTTLED SCULPIN

Cottus bairdii

Other Names: common sculpin, muddler, gudgeon

Habitat: cool, swift, hard-bottom streams or rocky or vegetated lakeshore

Range: eastern U.S. through Canada to the Hudson Bay and the Rocky Mountains; in Illinois, common in the upper tributaries of the Illinois-Fox River, rare in rest of the state

Food: aquatic invertebrates, fish eggs, small fish

Reproduction: spawns in late spring when water temperatures reach 63 to 73 degrees; male builds nest under ledge, log or stream bank then entices female with elaborate courtship displays; females turn upside down to deposit eggs on "roof" of nest; male attends nest through hatching

Average Size: 4 to 5 inches

Records: none

Notes: A fish of cool, fast streams that inhabits the same waters as Rainbow and Brown Trout, the Mottled Sculpin can tolerate somewhat warmer water than trout. Sculpins were once common in clear headwater streams, but populations have dwindled with the degradation of these streams. A frightening-looking fish, the Mottled Sculpin is perfectly harmless and forage for many top predators. In fact, Mottled Sculpins are a preferred baitfish for large Brown Trout. There are several species of deep-water sculpins native to the Great Lakes that are extinct or nearly so in Lake Michigan.

Description: sides bright silver to silver-green with conspicu-
ous light stripe; long thin body; upturned mouth; two
dorsal fins; tail deeply forked and pointed

Similar Species: Rainbow Smelt (pg. 134)

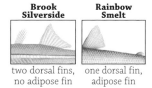

Brook Silverside	Rainbow Smelt
two dorsal fins, no adipose fin	one dorsal fin, adipose fin

BROOK SILVERSIDE

Atherinidae

Labidesthes sicculus

Other Names: northern silverside, skipjack, friar

Habitat: surface areas of clear lakes, slack water of large streams

Range: Great Lake states and the central U.S. south to the Gulf of Mexico; common throughout Illinois but not ubiquitous

Food: aquatic and flying insects, spiders

Reproduction: spawns in late spring and early summer; eggs are laid in sticky strings that are attached to vegetation

Average Size: 3 to 4 inches

Records: none

Notes: A member of a large family of tropical and subtropical mostly marine fish, the Brook Silverside is a flashy fish that is often seen cruising near the lake surface in small schools. Its upturned mouth is an adaptation to surface feeding. It's not uncommon to see Brook Silversides leap from the water, flying fish style, in pursuit of prey. Silversides have short life spans, lasting only 15 months. These sight feeders seem to become listless and feed less when the water becomes turbid.

Description: dark green back; silver to violet-blue sides; large mouth with prominent teeth; large eye; deeply forked tail; adipose fin

Similar Species: Alewife (pg. 56), Gizzard Shad (pg. 60), Skipjack Herring (pg. 58)

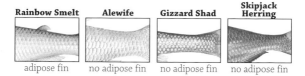

Rainbow Smelt	Alewife	Gizzard Shad	Skipjack Herring
adipose fin	no adipose fin	no adipose fin	no adipose fin

RAINBOW SMELT

Osmerus mordax

Other Names: ice or frost fish, lake herring, leefish

Habitat: open ocean and cool, medium depths of large lakes; tributary streams during spawning

Range: Coastal Pacific, Atlantic, and Arctic Oceans, land-locked lakes in southeastern Canada and the northeastern U.S.; in Illinois, Lake Michigan

Food: crustaceans, insect larvae, small fish

Reproduction: spawns in May, at night, in the first mile of tributary streams; a single female lays up to 50,000 eggs that are fertilized by several males waiting downstream; eggs sink and attach to the bottom on short pedestals

Average Size: 8 to 10 inches

Records: none

Notes: Smelt are marine fish that enter freshwater to spawn. A few northeastern lakes contain native populations. In 1912 fish from Maine were introduced into some Michigan lakes to support the introduced salmon stock. Smelt escaped into Lake Michigan and from there spread to the rest of the Great Lakes (except Lake Ontario where there is a native population). This small fish was soon making spectacular spawning runs in tributary streams and smelt fishing became a spring ritual. The Great Lakes smelt population crashed in the 1980s and has not fully recovered. Smelt are a good forage fish for large predators but consume sport fish fry and compete with them for food.

Description: mottled brown back and sides; torpedo-shaped body with very narrow caudal peduncle (area just before the tail); front portion of dorsal fin has four or five short separated spines; pelvic fin is abdominal and reduced to single fin; small, sharp teeth

Similar Species: Central Mudminnow (pg. 92)

Brook Stickleback	**Central Mudminnow**
spines in front of dorsal fin, slender body at base of tail	no spines, thick body at base of tail

BROOK STICKLEBACK

Culaea inconstans

Other Names: common or many-spined-stickleback, spiny minnow

Habitat: shallows of clear, cool streams and lakes

Range: Kansas through the northern U.S. and Canada; far northern Illinois and Lake Michigan

Food: small aquatic animals

Reproduction: male builds a golf ball-sized, globular nest of sticks and algae on submerged vegetation; female enters nest to deposit eggs then departs, often plowing a hole in the side in the process; male repairs nest and viciously guards the eggs until they hatch; ambitious males may build a second nest and move the eggs there

Average Size: 2 to 4 inches

Records: none

Notes: Most members of the stickleback family are marine fish but some are equally at home in freshwater or saltwater. There are four sticklebacks in the U.S., but only two in Illinois. These little fish are highly tolerant of alkaline and acidic conditions, but not turbidity, and are becoming rare over much of their range as water conditions deteriorate. The Brook Stickleback is restricted to streams in northern Illinois. These pugnacious little predators make fun aquarium fish, and will readily build and defend nests in captivity, though they may require live food when first captured.

Description: dark gray to black back; slate-gray to gray-green sides; bony plates on skin; tail shark-like, with upper lobe longer than lower; blunt snout with four barbels; spiracles (openings between eye and corner of gill)

Similar Species: Shovelnose Sturgeon (pg. 138)

Lake Sturgeon

spiracle between eye and gill

Shovelnose Sturgeon

lacks spiracles

LAKE STURGEON

Acipenser fulvescens

Acipenseridae

Other Names: rock, stone, red, black or smoothback sturgeon

Habitat: quiet waters in large rivers and lakes

Range: Hudson Bay, Great Lakes, Mississippi and Missouri drainages southeast to Alabama; in Illinois, Lake Michigan, and rarely the Mississippi and Illinois Rivers

Food: snails, clams, crayfish, aquatic insects

Reproduction: spawns from April through June in lake shallows and tributary streams; up to 1 million eggs are laid and fertilized a few at a time

Average Size: 3 to 5 feet, 5 to 40 pounds

Records: State—none; North American—168 pounds, Nattawasaga Lake, Ontario 1982

Notes: Sturgeons are one of the most primitive fish alive today, with relatives back more than 350 million years. They are bottom feeders that require clear, clean, deep lakes or river pools. They mature slowly, taking between ten and twenty years to spawn. Lake Sturgeon over three hundred pounds and a hundred years old have been reported in southern Canada. Lake Sturgeon were once so common in Lake Michigan that they filled commercial nets and were considered a trash fish and left on the shore. Today, they are not plentiful enough to be a sport fish in Illinois, but they are fished for in other states near the Great Lakes, including Minnesota and Wisconsin.

Description: copper-tan to light brown back and sides; long flat snout; bony plates instead of scales; shark-like tail, long upper lobe ending in long filament

Similar Species: Lake Sturgeon (pg. 138)

Shovelnose Sturgeon	Lake Sturgeon
lacks spiracles	spiracle between eye and gill

SHOVELNOSE STURGEON
Scaphirhynchus platorynchus

Other Names: hackleback, sand sturgeon, switchtail

Habitat: open, flowing channels of rivers and large streams with sand or gravel bottoms

Range: Hudson Bay south through the central U.S. west to New Mexico and east into Kentucky; native to all the larger Illinois Rivers, now only common in the Mississippi River

Food: clams, snails, crayfish, insects

Reproduction: spawns in spring when water temperatures reach 65 to 70 degrees; adults migrate upriver to dams or into small tributaries; eggs are deposited in swift current over gravel bars; spawns below dams when necessary

Average Size: 2 feet, 3 pounds

Records: State—8 pounds, 8.76 ounces, Rock River, Whiteside County, 2003; North American—8 pounds, 5 ounces, Rock River, Illinois, 1998

Notes: The Shovelnose Sturgeon is the smallest sturgeon in North America. This prehistoric-looking fish has cartilage instead of bones and hard plates instead of scales. They are now restricted to larger rivers, primarily the Mississippi, where it congregates below dams to spawn and are still netted commercially and the eggs are collected for caviar. The meat is oily, but very tasty when smoked. The Pallid Sturgeon, Illinois' only other sturgeon, is an exceedingly rare species occasionally caught in the Mississippi River between the Illinois and the Ohio Rivers.

141

Description: olive-brown to bronze back; dull olive-green sides fading to white belly; blunt snout; rounded head; long dorsal fin; large forward-facing mouth with thin lips; upper lip almost level with the eye

Similar Species: Black Buffalo (pg. 144), Common Carp (pg. 72), Smallmouth Buffalo (pg. 146)

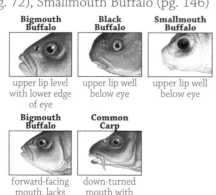

Bigmouth Buffalo
upper lip level with lower edge of eye

Black Buffalo
upper lip well below eye

Smallmouth Buffalo
upper lip well below eye

Bigmouth Buffalo
forward-facing mouth, lacks barbels

Common Carp
down-turned mouth with barbels

BIGMOUTH BUFFALO

Catostomidae

Ictiobus cyprinellus

Other Names: baldpate, blue router, mongrel, prairie or round buffalo, router

Habitat: soft-bottomed shallows of large lakes, sloughs and oxbows; slow-flowing rivers and streams

Range: Saskatchewan to Lake Erie south through the Mississippi River drainage to the Gulf of Mexico; common in the Mississippi, Illinois, Ohio and Wabash Rivers and their floodplain lakes

Food: small mollusks, aquatic insect larvae, zooplankton

Reproduction: spawns in early spring in clear, shallow water in flooded fields and marshes when water temperatures reach the low 60s; young quickly return to main lake or river when water recedes

Average Size: 18 to 20 inches, 10 to 12 pounds

Records: State—48 pounds, Mississippi River, Adams County, 1936; North American—73 pounds, 1 ounce, Lake Koshkonong, Wisconsin, 2004

Notes: This large, schooling fish is a filter feeder and commercially harvested with nets in the Mississippi, Illinois and Ohio Rivers but not often taken on hook and line. Bigmouth Buffalo can tolerate low oxygen levels, high water temperatures and some turbidity, but prefer clean, clear water to forage. This large, strong fighter is good to eat and would be a world-class sport fish if it would more readily take a hook.

143

Description: slate-green to dark gray back; sides have a blue-bronze sheen; deep body with a sloping back that supports a long dorsal fin; upper lip well below eye

Similar Species: Bigmouth Buffalo (pg. 142), Common Carp (pg. 72), Smallmouth Buffalo (pg. 146)

Bigmouth Buffalo

upper lip level with lower edge of eye

Black Buffalo

upper lip well below eye

Smallmouth Buffalo

upper lip well below eye

Bigmouth Buffalo

forward-facing mouth, lacks barbels

Common Carp

down turned mouth with barbels

BLACK BUFFALO

Ictiobus niger

Other Names: buoy tender, round, current or deep-water buffalo

Habitat: deep, fast water of large streams, deep sloughs, backwaters and impoundments

Range: lower Great Lakes and southern Mississippi River drainages west to South Dakota, south to New Mexico and Louisiana; in Illinois, the Mississippi, Illinois and Ohio Rivers, and sporadically in other large streams and flood plain lakes

Food: aquatic insects, crustaceans, algae

Reproduction: spawning takes place in April and May when water reaches the low 60s; adults move up tributaries to lay eggs in flooded sloughs and marshes

Average Size: 15 to 20 inches, 10 to 12 pounds

Records: State—23 pounds, 12 ounces, Rock River, 1984; North American—63 pounds, 6 ounces, Mississippi River, Iowa, 1999

Notes: The Black Buffalo is a southern species that inhabits the deep, strong currents of large rivers. Large numbers sometimes gather near buoys at the edge of channels. They were once very common in the Ohio and Scioto Rivers and were an important part of the commercial harvest. They are much less common now and seem to be affected by the invasion of Asian carp species. Though they are not often caught by anglers, Black Buffalo can be locally abundant and put up a tremendous fight in fast water. **145**

Description: slate green back with bronze sides; large dark eye; deep laterally compressed body; rounded head; blunt snout; small downturned mouth with thick lips

Similar Species: Black Buffalo (pg. 144), Bigmouth Buffalo (pg. 142), Common Carp (pg. 72)

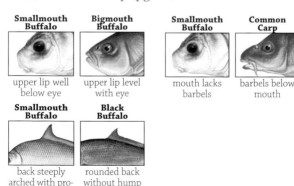

Smallmouth Buffalo	Bigmouth Buffalo	Smallmouth Buffalo	Common Carp
upper lip well below eye	upper lip level with eye	mouth lacks barbels	barbels below mouth

Smallmouth Buffalo	Black Buffalo
back steeply arched with pronounced hump	rounded back without hump

SMALLMOUTH BUFFALO

Ictiobus bubalus

Other Names: razorback, highback or humpback buffalo, thick-lipped buffalo

Habitat: moderate to swift currents in the deep, clean waters of larger streams and some lakes

Range: the Missouri, Mississippi and Ohio River drainages south to the Gulf and west into New Mexico; common in the large to midsized streams in Illinois and their flood plain lakes

Food: small mollusks, aquatic insect larvae and zooplankton

Reproduction: spawns in early spring in clear, shallow water of flooded fields and marshes when water temperatures reach the low 60s; young quickly return to main streams when water recedes

Average Size: 18 to 20 inches, 10 to 12 pounds

Records: State—48 pounds, Mississippi River, Adams County, 1936; North American—73 pounds, 1 ounce, Lake Koshkonong, Wisconsin, 2004

Notes: The smaller cousin of the Bigmouth Buffalo, the Smallmouth Buffalo is the most abundant buffalo in Illinois, but requires deeper, cleaner water and feeds more heavily on aquatic insect larvae. The Smallmouth Buffalo is commercially harvested and highly respected as table fare. It is often trucked live to markets on the coasts. Few Smallmouth Buffalo are caught by recreational anglers, but they are strong fighters when hooked.

147

Description: bright silver back and sides, often with yellow tinge; fins clear; deep body with round blunt head; leading edge of dorsal fin extends into a large, arching "quill"

Similar Species: Common Carp (pg. 72)

Quillback	**Common Carp**
mouth lacks barbels	barbels below mouth

QUILLBACK

Carpiodes cyprinus

Other Names: silver carp, carpsucker, lake quillback

Habitat: slow-flowing streams and rivers; backwaters and lakes, particularly areas with soft bottoms

Range: south-central Canada through the Great Lakes to the eastern U.S., south through the Mississippi drainage to the gulf; common in northern Illinois, less common in the south

Food: insects, plant matter, decaying material on bottom

Reproduction: spawns in late spring through early summer in tributaries or lake shallows; eggs are deposited in open areas over sand or mud

Average Size: 12 to 14 inches, 1 to 3 pounds

Records: State—none; North American—8 pounds, 13 ounces, Lake Winnebago, 2003

Notes: In North America, there are four fish known as carp-suckers. The Quillback is one of the three found in Illinois, and all are difficult to tell apart. Quillbacks prefer medium to large rivers and lakes and gather in schools as they filter feed along the bottom. Though they are not often sought after by anglers, they readily take wet flies and can be good fighters when caught on light tackle. The flesh is white and very flavorful.

149

Description: back brassy, green or gold; bronze, gold or green sides; off-white belly; dorsal and tail gray; lower fins yellow-orange to red; blunt nose with a sucker mouth; sickle-shaped dorsal fin

Similar Species: Northern Hog Sucker (pg. 154), Silver Redhorse (pg. 152), White Sucker (pg. 156)

Shorthead Redhorse

head small and slightly pointed

Silver Redhorse

large head with a blunt snout

Shorthead Redhorse

scales have dark spot where attached

Silver Redhorse

scales have dark edge, no dark spot where attached

Shorthead Redhorse

small head

Northern Hog Sucker

concave head between eyes

White Sucker

mouth even with snout

SHORTHEAD REDHORSE
Moxostoma macrolepidotum

Other Names: northern, golden, silver, greater, black or river redhorse

Habitat: clean streams and rivers with hard bottoms and clear lakes with strong-flowing tributary streams

Range: Central Canada and the U.S. through Atlantic states; common in Illinois except in the extreme south

Food: aquatic insects, small crustaceans and plant debris

Reproduction: spawns when the water reaches low 60s; adults migrate into small tributary streams to lay eggs on shallow gravel bars in swift currents near deep-water pools

Average Size: 18 to 24 inches, 2 to 5 pounds

Records: State—2 pounds, 2.56 ounces, Spoon River, Fulton County, 2003; North American—11 pounds, 5 ounces, Brunet River, Wisconsin, 1983

Notes: There are six varieties of redhorse in Illinois. The Shorthead, Golden and Silver are the largest, most common and widespread. All redhorses are "sucker type fish" and rather similar in appearance. They are clean-water fish and very susceptible to increased turbidity and pollutants. Redhorses are primarily stream fish; the Shorthead Redhorse is the exception, inhabiting a few lakes. They may all look alike but each is a separate species and occupies its own ecological niche. They are not important sport fish, but are caught fairly often by river anglers. They fight well on light tackle and are bony, but have good flavor when smoked.

151

Description: dark gray back, silver sides; silver-white belly; lower fins white or reddish-brown, red in breeding season; downturned sucker mouth; scales have a dark edge and no dark spot at point of attachment

Similar Species: Northern Hog Sucker (pg. 154), Shorthead Redhorse (pg. 150), White Sucker (pg. 156)

Silver Redhorse	**Shorthead Redhorse**	**Silver Redhorse**	**Shorthead Redhorse**
large head with a blunt snout	head small and slightly pointed	scales have a dark edge, but not dark corners	scales have dark spot at corners

SILVER REDHORSE

Moxostoma anisurum

Other Names: silver, bay, or redfin mullet, whitenose redhorse, longtail sucker

Habitat: clean streams and rivers with hard bottoms and
deep pools; a few clear lakes; shoals of Lake Michigan

Range: Manitoba to the St. Lawrence drainage south
to northern Alabama and Missouri; common in Lake
Michigan and the northern half of Illinois

Food: aquatic insects, small crustaceans and plant debris

Reproduction: spawns in early spring when the water
reaches the high 50s; adults migrate into small tributary
streams to lay eggs on shallow gravel bars in the swift
current near deep-water pools

Average Size: 11 to 22 inches, 2 to 5 pounds

Records: State—5 pounds, 10 ounces, Fox River, Kendall
County, 2003; North American—11 pounds, 5 ounces,
Brunet River, Wisconsin, 1983

Notes: Silver Redhorses are common in the large to medium
streams of northern and central Illinois. They prefer deep
pools and are readily caught with worms when fishing near
the bottom. The other redhorses are similar in appearance,
but each is a separate species and occupies its own niche.
Each redhorse has a distinctive lip shape and can be easily
told apart. All the redhorses require clean water with a hard
substrate and are declining in numbers with increased siltation. Redhorses are bony but have firm, flavorful flesh.

153

Description: back dark olive-brown fading to yellow-brown blotches on sides; 4 to 5 irregular dark saddles; elongated body almost round in cross-section; large head that is concave between the eyes; lower fins are dull red

Similar Species: Shorthead Redhorse (pg. 150), Silver Redhorse (pg. 152), White Sucker (pg. 156)

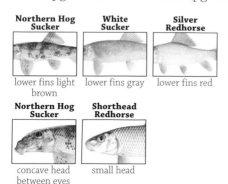

Northern Hog Sucker	White Sucker	Silver Redhorse
lower fins light brown	lower fins gray	lower fins red

Northern Hog Sucker	Shorthead Redhorse
concave head between eyes	small head

NORTHERN HOG SUCKER

Catostomidae

Hypentelium nigricans

Other Names: hog molly, hammerhead, riffle or bigheaded sucker, crawl-a-bottom

Habitat: riffles and tailwaters of clear streams with hard bottoms; found in a few lakes near the mouths of tributary streams

Range: central and eastern Canada and the U.S. south to Alabama and west to Oklahoma; common in clear streams in northeast Illinois and the Shawnee Hills in southern Illinois

Food: small crustaceans, aquatic insects

Reproduction: spawns when water reaches the low 60s; males gather in riffles or pools; females shed eggs that are fertilized by several males; no parental care

Average Size: 10 to 12 inches, 1 pound

Records: State—none; North American—1 pound, 12 ounces, Fox River, Wisconsin, 2004

Notes: Northern Hogsuckers are clean water fish well-adapted to feed in moving water. They use their elongated body structure and concave head to hold their place in riffles while turning over stones to release food. It is common for other fish to follow Hogsuckers to feed on what is stirred up. Northern Hogsuckers were once very common but have not fared well due to increased turbidity in many streams. Hog-suckers are not of much interest to anglers but are sometimes caught by fishermen working the edges of fast water.

155

Description: back olive to brownish; sides gray to silver; belly off-white; dorsal and tail fin slate; lower fins tinged orange; snout barely extends beyond upper lip; breeding males develop black or purple stripe

Similar Species: Northern Hog Sucker (pg. 154), Shorthead Redhorse (pg. 150), Silver Redhorse (pg. 152)

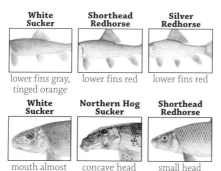

White Sucker	**Shorthead Redhorse**	**Silver Redhorse**
lower fins gray, tinged orange	lower fins red	lower fins red

White Sucker	**Northern Hog Sucker**	**Shorthead Redhorse**
mouth almost even with snout	concave head between eyes	small head

WHITE SUCKER

Catostomus commersoni

Other Names: common, coarse-scaled or eastern sucker, bay fish, black mullet

Habitat: clear to turbid (cloudy) streams, rivers and lakes

Range: Canada throughout the east-central U.S. and south from New Mexico to South Carolina; common throughout Illinois

Food: insects, crustaceans, plant material

Reproduction: spawns in early spring when water reaches the high 50s to low 60s; adults spawn in tributary riffles over gravel or coarse sand; in lakes, eggs are deposited over shallow gravel or rocks along wave-swept shorelines

Average Size: 12 to 18 inches, 1 to 3 pounds

Records: State—none; North American—7 pounds, 4 ounces, Big Round Lake, Wisconsin, 1978

Notes: The white sucker is one of the most widespread fish in Illinois and one of the most important. Highly productive, it provides a large source of forage for game fish and is a mainstay in the bait industry. White suckers thrive in most habitats, even heavily-silted streams in Illinois' agricultural areas. There is a good population in Lake Michigan where they can be very evident in the shallows when spawning. White Suckers are not often sought after by anglers in Illinois but have firm, good-tasting flesh that is prized by some when smoked.

157

Description: dark green back; greenish sides often with dark lateral band; large forward-facing mouth; lower jaw extends to rear margin of eye

Similar Species: Smallmouth Bass (pg. 160), Spotted Bass (pg. 162)

Largemouth Bass	Smallmouth Bass	Spotted Bass
mouth extends well beyond non-red eye	mouth does not extend beyond red eye	mouth does not extend beyond the eye

LARGEMOUTH BASS

Micropterus salmoides

Other Names: black, bayou, green or slough bass, green trout

Habitat: shallow, fertile, weedy lakes and river backwaters; weedy bays of large lakes

Range: southern Canada through the United States into Mexico, extensively introduced throughout the world; common throughout Illinois

Food: small fish, frogs, crayfish, insects

Reproduction: spawning takes place in May and June when water temperatures reach 60 degrees; male builds a nest in a weedbed less than 6 feet deep; male fans and guards the nest until the "brood swarm" disperses

Average Size: 12 to 20 inches, 1 to 5 pounds

Records: State—13 pounds, 1 ounce, Stone Quarry Lake, Lake County, 1976; North American—22 pounds, 4 ounces, Montgomery Lake, Georgia, 1932

Notes: The Largemouth Bass is the most sought after game fish in North America. This denizen of the weeds is a voracious carnivore, eating anything that is alive and will fit into its mouth. Largemouths are native to most of Illinois and were stocked in any waters that would sustain them. Largemouth Bass run one to two pounds, with six and seven pounders not uncommon in Illinois. They are quite tasty when small and taken from clean water, but tend to be slightly mud-flavored when taken from silty water.

Description: back and sides mottled dark green to bronze or pale gold, often with dark vertical bands; white belly; stout body; large, forward-facing mouth; red eyes

Similar Species: Largemouth Bass (pg. 158), Spotted Bass (pg. 162)

Smallmouth Bass	Largemouth Bass		Smallmouth Bass	Spotted Bass

mouth does not extend beyond red eye	mouth extends well beyond non-red eye		vertical bars on sides	lateral stripe on sides

SMALLMOUTH BASS

Micropterus dolomieui

Other Names: bronzeback, redeye bass, redeye, white or mountain trout

Habitat: clear, swift-flowing streams and rivers; clear lakes with gravel or rocky shorelines

Range: introduced throughout North America, Europe and Asia; common in northern Illinois, rare in the south

Food: insects, small fish, crayfish

Reproduction: male builds nest in 3 to 10 feet of water on open gravel beds when water temperatures reach the mid-to-high 60s; nest is often near a log or boulder; male aggressively guards the nest and young until fry disperse

Average Size: 12 to 20 inches, 1 to 4 pounds

Records: State—6 pounds, 7 ounces, Strip Mine, Fulton County, 1995; North American—11 pounds, 15 ounces, Dale Hollow Lake, Tennessee, 1955

Notes: The Smallmouth Bass is a world-class game fish noted for its strong fighting ability and spectacular leaps. Native to the state, it is primarily a stream fish in the northern two thirds of Illinois, but is also found in some clear impoundments. Overfishing, dammed streams and decreased water quality have reduced the Smallmouth population in Illinois. Smallmouth Bass prefer deep, open water more than its larger cousin, and it is often found in deep pools at the current's edge. The flesh is firm, succulent, and regarded by some anglers as second only to Lake Trout and Whitefish.

161

Description: dark green back fading to lighter green sides; diamond-shaped blotches form a dark stripe on side; dark spots above the stripe; light spots on base of each scale below stripe; dark lines extend from reddish eye

Similar Species: Largemouth Bass (pg. 158), Smallmouth Bass (pg. 160)

mouth does not extend beyond the eye

mouth extends beyond non-red eye

spotting below lateral line

vertical bars on sides

SPOTTED BASS

Micropterus punctulatus

Other Names: Kentucky, speckled or yellow bass, spot

Habitat: deeper silted pools in sluggish, medium-to-large streams; larger lakes and reservoirs

Range: the Ohio and Mississippi drainage in the southern U.S. from Florida to Texas; the Illinois, Wabash and Mississippi River drainages in southeastern Illinois

Food: small fish, crayfish

Reproduction: male builds a nest in open gravel beds three to four feet deep from May to June when water temperatures reach mid-to-high 60s; male aggressively guards the nest and young

Average Size: 8 to 18 inches, 8 ounces to 2 pounds

Records: State—7 pounds, 3.12 ounces, Strip Mine, Fulton County, 1992; North American—10 pounds, 4 ounces, Pine Flat Lake, California, 2001

Notes: This bass is primarily a stream fish but has done well in large impoundments, particularly Illinois' flooded strip mines. In terms of habits, Spotted Bass fall between Largemouth and Smallmouth Bass. Whereas Smallmouths seek stream riffles and Largemouths the edges of weed-beds, Spotted Bass prefer slow, deep pools. In reservoirs, they seek deeper water than Smallmouth Bass. Spotted Bass are smaller fish than Largemouths but frequently larger than Illinois' Smallmouth Bass.

Description: black to olive back; silver sides with dark green to black blotches; its back is more arched and the depression above the eye is more pronounced than in the White Crappie

Similar Species: White Crappie (pg. 166)

Black Crappie	White Crappie	Black Crappie	White Crappie
usually 7 to 8 spines in dorsal fin	usually 5 to 6 spines in dorsal fin	dorsal fin length equal to the distance from the dorsal to the eye	dorsal fin shorter than the distance from the eye to the dorsal

164

BLACK CRAPPIE

Centrarchidae

Pomoxis nigromaculatus

Other Names: speck, speckled perch, papermouth

Habitat: quiet, clear water of streams and midsized lakes; often associated with vegetation but may roam deep, open basins and flats, particularly during winter

Range: southern Manitoba through the Atlantic and south-eastern states, introduced but not common in the West; common throughout Illinois

Food: small fish, aquatic insects, zooplankton

Reproduction: spawns in shallow weedbeds from May to June when water temperatures reach the high 50s; male builds circular nest in fine gravel or sand, then guards eggs and young until fry begin feeding

Average Size: 7 to 12 inches, 5 ounces to 1 pound

Records: State—4 pounds, 11 ounces, private lake, Jennings County, 1994; North American—6 pounds, Westwego Canal, Louisiana, 1969

Notes: Crappies are the most popular Illinois panfish in all seasons, as they feed actively in both winter and summer. They are sought for their sweet-tasting white fillets, but not for their fighting ability. Black Crappies nest in colonies and often gather in large feeding schools. Widespread in Illinois, Black Crappies occupy most waters that are clear with good vegetation and little current. Black Crappies require clearer water and more vegetation than White Crappies and are decreasing in numbers with increased siltation in many Illinois lakes.

Description: greenish back; silvery green to white sides with 7 to 9 dark vertical bars; the only sunfish with six spines in both the dorsal and anal fin

Similar Species: Black Crappie (pg. 164)

White Crappie

Black Crappie

usually 5 to 6 spines in dorsal fin

usually 7 to 8 spines in dorsal fin

White Crappie

Black Crappie

dorsal fin shorter than the distance from the eye to the dorsal

dorsal fin length equal to the distance from the dorsal to the eye

WHITE CRAPPIE

Centrarchidae

Pomoxis annularis

Other Names: silver, pale or ringed crappie, papermouth

Habitat: slightly silty streams and midsize lakes; prefers less vegetation than the Black Crappie

Range: North Dakota south and east to the Gulf and Atlantic states except peninsular Florida; common throughout Illinois

Food: aquatic insects, small fish, plankton

Reproduction: spawns on firm sand or gravel when the water temperature approaches 60 degrees; male builds a shallow, round nest, and guards eggs and young after spawning

Average Size: 8 to 10 inches, 5 ounces to 1 pound

Records: State—4 pounds, 7 ounces, private pond, Morgan County, 1973; North American—5 pounds, 3 ounces, Enid Dam, Mississippi, 1957

Notes: The southern cousin of the Black Crappie, the White Crappie is native to Illinois and common throughout the state. They prefer deeper, less vegetated, and more turbid (cloudy) water than Black Crappies. Due to its acceptance of turbid water, there is some indication of a positive relationship between Common Carp and White Crappie. Black and White Crappies can be found in mixed schools during the winter and they occasionally interbreed. Both actively feed during the winter and at night.

Description: dark olive to green on back, blending to silver-gray, copper, orange, purple or brown on sides; 5 to 9 dark vertical bars on sides that fade with age; yellow belly and copper breast; large dark gill spot that extends completely to gill margin; dark spot on rear margin of dorsal fin

Similar Species: Green Sunfish (pg. 170), Pumpkinseed (pg. 176), Redear Sunfish (pg. 178)

Bluegill	Green Sunfish		Bluegill	Pumpkinseed

small mouth · large mouth · · short pointed pectoral fins · long pointed pectoral fins

Bluegill	Pumpkinseed	Redear

dark gill spot · red/orange margin on gill spot · red/orange margin on gill spot

BLUEGILL

Centrarchidae

Lepomis macrochirus

Other Names: bream, sun perch, blue sunfish, copperbelly, strawberry bass

Habitat: medium to large streams and most lakes with weedy bays or shorelines

Range: southern Canada through the southern states into Mexico; common throughout Illinois

Food: aquatic insects, snails, small fish

Reproduction: spawns from late May to early August when water temperatures reach the high 60s to low 80s; male builds a nest in shallow, sparse vegetation in a colony of up to 50 other nests; male guards nest and fry

Average Size: 6 to 9 inches, 5 to 8 ounces

Records: State—3 pounds, 8 ounces, private pond, Jasper County, 1987; North American—4 pounds, 12 ounces, Ketona Lake, Alabama, 1950

Notes: Bluegills are native to Illinois and are common throughout the state. They are one of the most popular panfish in Illinois and in the United States. Bluegills prefer impoundments and are not often found in streams with much current, but they do frequent the backwaters of large rivers. Bluegills prefer deep weedbeds at the edge of open water. They have small mouths and feed mostly on insects and small fish on the surface. Bluegills are popular with fly-fishermen, and many lakes have large populations of hybrid sunfish, crosses between Bluegills and Green or Pumpkinseed Sunfish.

Description: dark green back; dark olive to bluish sides; yellow to cream belly; scales flecked with yellow, producing a brassy appearance; dark gill spot with pale margin; large mouth with thick lips

Similar Species: Bluegill (pg. 168), Pumpkinseed (pg. 176), Redear Sunfish (pg. 178)

Green Sunfish	Bluegill	Pumpkinseed	Redear Sunfish
dark gill spot has a pale margin	round gill spot with clear margin	red/orange margin on gill spot	red/orange margin on gill spot

Green Sunfish	Pumpkin Seed	Redear Sunfish
faint blue stripes on head	blue stripes on head	no blue stripes on head

GREEN SUNFISH
Lepomis cyanellus

Other Names: green perch, sand bass

Habitat: weedy, warm, shallow lakes and backwaters of slow-moving streams

Range: most of the United States into Mexico excluding Florida and the Rocky Mountains; found throughout Illinois

Food: aquatic insects, small crustaceans, fish

Reproduction: male builds nest in less than a foot of weedy water; spawns in temperatures from 60 to 80 degrees; may produce two broods per year; male guards nest and fans eggs until hatching

Average Size: 4 to 6 inches, less than 8 ounces

Records: State—2 pounds, 1 ounce, private pond, Dewitt County, 1981; North American—2 pounds, 2 ounces, Stockton Lake, Missouri, 1971

Notes: Green Sunfish are often mistaken for Bluegills but prefer shallower weedbeds. They are very tolerant of turbid water and low oxygen levels, and they thrive in warm, weedy lakes and backwaters. They have become very common in Illinois, outcompeting other sunfish. Green Sunfish stunt easily, filling some lakes with 3-inch-long "potato chips." Green Sunfish hybridize with Bluegills and Pumpkinseeds, producing large, aggressive offspring.

Description: dark greenish-blue back; sides light green and flecked with blue or yellow; belly and chest are bright orange to pale yellow; gill flap tapers into a long, black finger with a red margin

Similar Species: Redear Sunfish (pg. 178)

Longear Sunfish	Redear Sunfish	Longear Sunfish	Redear Sunfish
dark spots on dorsal fin	no spots on dorsal fin	blue-green bands on side of head	solid green to bronze head

LONGEAR SUNFISH

Centrarchidae

Lepomis megalotis

Other Names: Great Lakes longear, blue-and-orange sunfish, red perch

Habitat: clear, moderately weedy, slow-moving shallow streams, and quiet, clear lakes

Range: central states north to Quebec, east to the Appalachian Mountains and as far south as the Gulf of Mexico, introduced into some western states; common in southeastern Illinois

Food: small insects, crustaceans, fish

Reproduction: male builds and guards nest on shallow gravel bed when water temperatures reach the mid-70s

Average Size: 3 to 4 inches, 5 ounces

Records: State—none; North American—1 pound, 12 ounces, Big Round Lake, New Mexico

Notes: Longears are bright, secretive little sunfish that prefer clear, slow-moving shallow streams, but they do inhabit some clean Illinois lakes. This southern species reaches the limits of its range in the southern Great Lakes region. These sunfish require clean water and are disappearing from many streams due to increased siltation from agricultural runoff. Longears feed on the surface more than other sunfish. There is some hybridization between Longears and other sunfish.

Description: blue-green back fading to orange; about 30 orange or red spots on sides of males, brown spots on females; orange pelvic and anal fins; black gill spot with light margin

Similar Species: Pumpkinseed Sunfish (pg. 176), Redear Sunfish (pg. 178)

Orangespotted Sunfish

light margin on gill spot

Pumpkinseed

orange or red crescent on gill flap

Redear Sunfish

orange or red crescent on gill

Orangespotted Sunfish

rounded pectoral fin

Redear Sunfish

pointed pectoral fin

ORANGESPOTTED SUNFISH

Centrarchidae

Lepomis humilis

Other Names: orangespot, dwarf sunfish, pygmy sunfish

Habitat: open to moderately weedy pools with soft bottoms

Range: from the southern Great Lakes through the Mississippi River basin to the Gulf states; locally abundant in lakes and streams throughout Illinois

Food: small insects, crustaceans

Reproduction: male builds and guards nest in shallow, weedy water when temperatures reach the mid 60s; colonial nesters with 50 or more nests together in a colony

Average Size: 3 to 4 inches, 4 ounces

Records: none

Notes: This brightly colored sunfish is too small to be an important panfish in Illinois. They tolerate a wide variety of habitats except fast-moving streams. They survive well in silty water and tolerate slight pollution, making them well suited for small lakes in agricultural areas. Orangespotted Sunfish are important as forage for other game fish and may be important for mosquito larvae control in some areas. They make beautiful aquarium fish but may require some live food.

Description: back brown to olive fading to light olive; sides speckled with orange-yellow spots, with 7 to 10 vertical bands; black gill spot with light margin and orange crescent

Similar Species: Bluegill (pg. 168), Green Sunfish (pg. 170), Redear Sunfish (pg. 178)

blue stripes on head

no blue stripes on head

long, pointed pectoral fin

rounded pectoral fin

orange or red crescent on gill flap

gill spot lacks light margin

orange or red crescent on gill

PUMPKINSEED

Centrarchidae

Lepomis gibbosus

Other Names: round or yellow sunfish, punky, sun bass, bream

Habitat: weedy ponds, lakes, reservoirs and slow-moving streams; prefers slightly cooler water than Bluegills

Range: central and eastern North America, introduced in the West; common in northern Illinois

Food: snails, insects, small fish

Reproduction: spawns from late May to August when water temperatures reach 55 to 63 degrees; male builds nest among weeds in less than 2 feet of water with a sand or gravel bottom; male aggressively guards the nest; may produce multiple broods

Average Size: 6 to 8 inches, 5 to 8 ounces

Records: State—none; North American—2 pounds, 4 ounces, North Saluda River, South Carolina, 1997

Notes: This small, brightly colored sunfish is one of Illinois' most beautiful fish. Pumpkinseeds are a northern sunfish that is native to the natural lakes and quiet streams in northeastern Illinois. Pumpkinseeds often gather in small schools around docks and submerged deadfalls. They readily hybridize with other sunfish and the hybrids may totally colonize some lakes. They have specialized teeth for feeding on snails. Pumpkinseeds eagerly attack natural and artificial bait and are fine table fare.

Description: back and sides bronze to dark green, fading to light green; faint vertical bars; bluish stripes on side of head; gill flap short with dark spot and red margin in males

Similar Species: Pumpkinseed (pg. 176), Longear Sunfish (pg. 172)

Redear Sunfish

solid green to bronze head lacks blue lines

Longear Sunfish

blue-green bands on side of head

Pumpkinseed

wavy blue lines on head

Redear Sunfish

no spots on dorsal fin

Longear Sunfish

dark spots on dorsal fin

REDEAR SUNFISH

Centrarchidae

Lepomis microlophus

Other Names: shellcracker, stumpknocker, yellow bream

Habitat: congregates around stumps and logs in low to moderate vegetation in large, quiet lakes, and introduced into farm ponds

Range: northern Midwest through the southern states, introduced into the northern and western states; commonly stocked throughout Illinois

Food: mainly mollusks

Reproduction: male builds and guards nest in shallow, weedy water in May and June when water temperatures reach the high 60s; may produce second brood well into the summer

Average size: 8 to 10 inches, 8 ounces to 1 pound

Records: State—2 pounds, 12 ounces, Marion CC Lake, Williamson County, 1985; North America—5 pounds, 7.5 ounces, Diversion Canal, South Carolina, 1998

Notes: The Redear Sunfish is a large, highly regarded panfish of the South that is native to southeastern Illinois and is now stocked throughout the state. The introduction of this large, aggressive sunfish was very successful and Redears are now one of the most popular panfish in Illinois. Redears prefer warmer water than other Illinois sunfish, and are aggressive feeders in summer. They are not as active as Bluegills in winter, but they can be caught through the ice.

Description: brown to olive green back and sides with overall bronze appearance; each scale on the sides has a dark spot; red eye; thicker, heavier body than other sunfish; large mouth

Similar Species: Bluegill (pg. 168), Green Sunfish (pg. 170), Warmouth (pg. 182)

Rock Bass
large mouth extends to eye

Bluegill
small mouth does not extend to eye

Rock Bass
lacks red-brown streaks radiating from eye

Warmouth
red-brown streaks radiate from eye

Rock Bass
6 spines in anal fin

Green Sunfish
3 spines in anal fin

ROCK BASS

Ambloplites rupestris

Other Names: redeye, goggle eye, rock sunfish

Habitat: vegetation on rocky bottoms in clearwater lakes and medium-sized streams

Range: southern Canada through central and eastern United States to the edge of the Gulf states; common in eastern Illinois and Lake Michigan, sporadic in western Illinois

Food: prefers crayfish, but eats aquatic insects and small fish

Reproduction: spawns when water temperatures are in the high 60s and 70s; male builds nest in coarse gravel in submerged vegetation less than 3 feet deep; male guards eggs and fry

Average Size: 8 to 10 inches, 8 ounces to 1 pound

Records: State—1 pound, 10 ounces, Aux Sable Lake, Grundy County, 1987; North American—3 pounds, York River, Ontario, 1974

Notes: This large sunfish is native to the Illinois River and was once found in almost every stream, but was less common in inland lakes. Rock Bass require cool well-oxygenated water and are declining in numbers with increased siltation in many streams. Rock Bass are good fighters and are frequently caught, but not often sought after by fishermen. In both lakes and streams, Rock Bass are normally found over a rocky or gravel substrate, even when vegetation is present. They are frequently found in schools that stay put, not moving from their home territories. Once these schools are located, Rock Bass are easy to catch.

181

Description: back and sides greenish gray to brown, lightly mottled with faint vertical bands; stout body; large mouth; red eyes; 3 to 5 reddish-brown streaks radiate from eyes

Similar Species: Bluegill (pg. 168), Green Sunfish (pg. 170), Pumpkinseed (pg. 176), Rock Bass (pg. 180)

Warmouth	Bluegill	Green Sunfish
jaw extends at least to middle of eye	small mouth does not extend to eye	jaw does not extend to middle of eye

Warmouth	Pumpkinseed	Rock Bass
light margin on gill spot	orange or red crescent on gill flap	dark gill spot lacks light margin

WARMOUTH

Lepomis gulosus

Other Names: goggle eye, widemouth sunfish, stump-knocker, weed bass

Habitat: heavy weeds in turbid (cloudy) lakes, swamps and slow-moving streams

Range: southern U.S. from Texas to Florida north to the southern Great Lakes region; common in southeastern Illinois and the Illinois River basin, infrequent in central and northwestern Illinois

Food: crayfish, aquatic insects and small fish

Reproduction: spawns when water temperatures are in the high 60s and 70s; male builds a nest in coarse gravel in submerged vegetation less than 3 feet deep; male guards eggs and fry

Average Size: 11 inches, 8 to 12 ounces

Records: State—1 pound, 13 ounces, private pond, Cumberland County, 1971; North American—2 pounds, 7 ounces, Yellow River, Florida, 1985

Notes: With the draining of wetlands, this secretive sunfish is less common in Illinois than it once was. Warmouths are solitary, aggressive sight feeders that are often found near rocks and submerged stumps when not hiding in dense vegetation. They prefer cloudy water with a soft bottom and can withstand low oxygen levels, high silt loads and temperatures into the 90s. Its small size keeps it off the radar of most fishermen, but it has a good flavor and is a scrappy, strong fighter on light tackle.

183

Description: dark gray back; bright silver sides with 7 or 8 indistinct or broken stripes; dorsal fin separated, front part hard spines rear part soft rays; two tooth patches, one on back of the tongue

Similar Species: Striped Bass (pg. 188), White Bass (pg. 186), Yellow Bass (pg. 190)

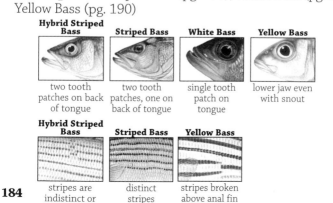

Hybrid Striped Bass	**Striped Bass**	**White Bass**	**Yellow Bass**
two tooth patches on back of tongue	two tooth patches, one on back of tongue	single tooth patch on tongue	lower jaw even with snout

Hybrid Striped Bass	**Striped Bass**	**Yellow Bass**
stripes are indistinct or broken	distinct stripes	stripes broken above anal fin

HYBRID STRIPED BASS

Morone saxatilis X Morone chrysops

Other Names: white striper, wiper

Habitat: open water of large lakes and slow-moving rivers

Range: stocked in about 40 U.S. states; stocked in Illinois' larger lakes and reservoirs

Food: small fish

Reproduction: hatchery-produced hybrid that is only occasionally fertile

Average Size: 18 to 20 inches, 8 to 10 pounds

Records: State—20 pounds, .32 ounces, Lake of Egypt, Johnson County, 2004; North American—27 pounds, 5 ounces, Greer's Ferry Lake, Arkansas, 1997

Notes: The Striped Bass Hybrid is a hatchery hybrid and most often a cross between a female Striped Bass and a male White Bass. They do not reproduce but may interbreed with the parent stock. Illinois now raises large numbers of fingerlings to stock in impoundments too warm to support Striped Bass. This hard-fighting, tasty bass has now become a favorite with anglers in Illinois and across the country. The Hybrid Striped Bass is also becoming an important aquaculture fish, supplying fillets for the grocery store and the restaurant market.

Description: gray-black back; silver sides with 6 to 8 black stripes; front hard-spined portion of dorsal fin separated from soft-rayed rear portion; mouth protrudes beyond snout

Similar Species: Hybrid Striped Bass (pg. 184), Striped Bass (pg. 188), White Bass (pg. 186), Yellow Bass (pg. 190)

White Bass	Hybrid Striped Bass	Striped Bass	Yellow Bass
faded, incomplete stripes	stripes indistinct or broken	distinct stripes	stripes broken above anal fin

White Bass	Hybrid Striped Bass	Striped Bass
one tooth patch on front of tongue	two tooth patches, one on back of tongue	two tooth patches on back of tongue

WHITE BASS
Morone chrysops

Other Names: lake, sand or silver bass, streaker

Habitat: large lakes, rivers and impoundments with relatively clear water

Range: the Great Lakes region to the eastern seaboard, through the southeast to the Gulf and west to Texas; common in Illinois' larger rivers and impoundments, but not southern Lake Michigan

Food: small fish

Reproduction: spawns in late spring or early summer; eggs spread in open water over gravel beds or rubble 6 to 10 feet deep; some populations migrate to narrow bays or up tributary streams to spawn

Average Size: 18 inches, 8 ounces to 2 pounds

Records: State—4 pounds, 14 ounces, Kaskaskia River, Clinton County, 1981; North American—6 pounds, 13 ounces, Lake Orange, Virginia, 1989

Notes: The White Bass is native to Lake Michigan and larger rivers in Illinois and now has been stocked in other impoundments. White Bass are only infrequently found in southern Lake Michigan. This popular fish inhabits large lakes and rivers where they travel in schools near the surface. White Bass can often be spotted by watching for seagulls feeding on baitfish driven to the surface by schools of bass. The flesh is somewhat soft but has a good flavor and can be improved if it is put on ice as soon as it is caught.

Description: dark gray back; bright silver sides with 7 or 8 distinct stripes; two tooth patches; dorsal fin separated, front part hard spines, rear part soft rays

Similar Species: Hybrid Striped Bass (pg. 184), White Bass (pg. 186), Yellow Bass (pg. 190)

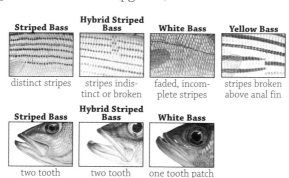

Striped Bass	Hybrid Striped Bass	White Bass	Yellow Bass
distinct stripes	stripes indistinct or broken	faded, incomplete stripes	stripes broken above anal fin

Striped Bass	Hybrid Striped Bass	White Bass
two tooth patches, one on back of tongue	two tooth patches, one on back of tongue	one tooth patch on front of tongue

STRIPED BASS

Moronidae

Morone saxatilis

Other Names: striper, streaker, surf bass, rockfish

Habitat: coastal oceans and associated spawning streams; landlocked in some large lakes

Range: the Atlantic coast from Maine to northern Florida, the Gulf Coast from Florida to Texas and introduced to the Pacific coast and some large inland impoundments; in Illinois, stocked in a few larger lakes and reservoirs, some escapees found in larger rivers

Food: small fish

Reproduction: spawns in late spring to early summer in freshwater streams; eggs deposited in riffles at the mouth of large tributaries; eggs must remain suspended to hatch

Average Size: 18 to 30 inches, 10 to 20 pounds

Records: State—31 pounds, 7 ounces, Stangchris Lake, Christian County, 1994; North American—78 pounds, 8 ounces, Atlantic City, New Jersey, 1992

Notes: The Striped Bass is a saltwater fish that migrates into freshwater to spawn. In the early 1960s, it was discovered that Striped Bass could live entirely in freshwater. Large numbers were soon being reared in hatcheries and stocked in many southern and western lakes and rivers. These introduced populations cannot reproduce naturally and must be maintained through stocking. Only a limited number of Striped Bass were stocked in Illinois before stocking efforts shifted to Hybrid Striped Bass, which fare better in Illinois' warm water.

189

Description: silvery yellow to brassy sides with 6 or 7 black stripes broken just above anal fin; yellowish-white belly; forked tail; two sections of dorsal fin connected by membrane

Similar Species: Hybrid Striped Bass (pg. 184), Striped Bass (pg. 188), White Bass (pg. 186)

Yellow Bass	**Hybrid Striped Bass**	**Striped Bass**	**White Bass**

stripes broken above anal fin	stripes indistinct or broken	distinct stripes	faded, incomplete stripes

Yellow Bass	**White Bass**
lower jaw even with snout	jaw protrudes beyond snout

YELLOW BASS

Morone mississippiensis

Other Names: brassy or gold bass, barfish

Habitat: open water over shallow gravel bars in lakes and pools in larger rivers

Range: the Great Lakes region to the eastern seaboard, through the southeast to the Gulf and west to Texas; locally abundant in lower Illinois and upper Mississippi Rivers and lakes in the northeast

Food: small fish, insects, and crustaceans

Reproduction: spawns in late spring over gravel bars in the mouths of tributary streams

Average Size: 8 to 12 inches, eight ounces to 1 pound

Records: State—2 pounds, private pond, Madison County, 1994; North American—6 pounds, 13 ounces, Lake Orange, Virginia, 1989

Notes: The Yellow Bass is a close cousin to the White Bass. It was once thought to be more abundant in Illinois than the White Bass, but is now only common in a few lakes and the lower Illinois River. Its schooling and feeding habits are similar to the White Bass but it tends to stay in the middle of the water column or near the bottom. The Yellow Bass is a popular panfish in some areas where its flaky, white flesh is considered superior to that of White Bass.

Description: back and sides yellow-brown with slight cross-hatching; dark lateral stripe through lips to tail; slender fish with pelvic, dorsal and anal fins set well back on body; tail, dorsal and anal fins spotted; long snout flattened on top; rounded tail; upturned mouth

Similar Species: Brook Silverside (pg. 132), Central Mudminnow (pg. 92)

Blackstripe Topminnow	Brook Silverside	Central Mudminnow
spotted tail, dorsal and anal fins, one dorsal fin	long anal fin with a straight or concave edge, two dorsal fins	short anal fin with a straight or concave edge, two dorsal fins

192

BLACKSTRIPE TOPMINNOW

Fundulidae

Fundulus notatus

Other Names: blackband topminnow

Habitat: slow-moving streams, quiet margins and backwaters of medium-sized rivers, small lakes and ponds

Range: southern Great Lakes through the central Mississippi River drainage to the Gulf; common throughout Illinois except the Shawnee Hills

Food: insects, crustaceans

Reproduction: spawns when water reaches the low 70s; pairs establish territory along stream edges; male aggressively defends territory; eggs sink to the bottom and are left without parental care

Average Size: 2 to 3 inches

Records: none

Notes: As the name implies "topminnows" inhabit the upper water column and are adapted to feeding on, or near, the surface. Though inconspicuous and well camouflaged, they are the favorite target of wading birds. They tolerate turbid water well and are now becoming common in manmade farm ponds and waters where few other fish survive. Top-minnows arc attractive fish and fun to watch, and even though they are not very colorful, they make good aquarium fish and readily eat food spread on the water's surface.

GLOSSARY

adipose fin a small, fleshy fin without rays, located on the midline of the fish's back between the dorsal fin and the tail

air bladder a balloon-like organ located in the gut area of a fish, used to control buoyancy—and in the respiration of some species such as gar; also called "swim bladder" or "gas bladder"

alevin a newly hatched fish that still has its yolk sac

anadromous a fish that hatches in freshwater, migrates to the ocean, then re-enters streams or rivers from the sea (or large inland body of water) to spawn

anal fin a single fin located on the bottom of the fish near the tail

annulus marks or rings on the scales, spine, vertebrae or otoliths that scientists use to determine a fish's age

anterior toward the front of a fish, opposite of posterior

bands horizontal marks running lengthwise along the side of a fish

barbel thread-like sensory structures on a fish's head often near the mouth, commonly called "whiskers;" used for taste or smell

bars vertical markings on the side of a fish

benthic organisms living in or on the bottom

brood swarm large group of young fish such as bullheads

cardiform teeth small teeth on the lips of a catfish

carnivore a fish that feeds on other fish or animals

catadromous a fish that lives in freshwater and migrates into saltwater to spawn, such as the American Eel

caudal fin tail fin

caudal peduncle the portion of the fish's body located between the anal fin and the beginning of the tail

coldwater referring to a species or environment; in fish, often a species of trout or salmon found in water that rarely exceeds 70 degrees; also used to describe a lake or river according to average summer temperature

copepod a small (less than 2 mm) crustacean that is part of the zooplankton community

crustacean a crayfish, water flea, crab or other animal belonging to group of mostly aquatic species that have paired antennae, jointed legs and an exterior skeleton (exoskeleton); common food for many fish

dorsal relating to the top of the fish, on or near the back; opposite of the ventral, or lower, part of the fish

dorsal fin the fin or fins located along the top of a fish's back

eddy a circular water current, often created by an obstruction

epilimnion the warm, oxygen-rich upper layer of water in a thermally stratified lake

exotic a foreign species, not native to a watershed

fingerling a juvenile fish, generally 1 to 10 inches in length, in its first year of life

fork length the overall length of a fish from the mouth to the deepest part of the tail notch

fry recently hatched young fish that have absorbed their yolk sacs

game fish a species regulated by laws for recreational fishing

gills organs used in aquatic respiration

gill cover large bone covering the gills, also called opercle or operculum

gill raker a comb-like projection from the gill arch

harvest fish that are caught and kept by sport or commercial anglers

hypolimnion bottom layer of water in a thermally stratified lake (common in summer), usually depleted of oxygen by decaying matter

ichthyologist a scientist who studies fish

invertebrates animals without backbones, such as insects, crayfish, leeches and earthworms

lateral line a series of pored scales along the side of a fish that contain organs used to detect vibrations

littoral zone the part of a lake that is less than 15 feet in depth; this important and often vulnerable area holds the majority of aquatic plants, is a primary area used by young fish, and offers essential spawning habitat for most warmwater fishes such as Walleye and Largemouth Bass

mandible lower jaw

maxillary upper jaw

milt semen of a male fish that fertilizes the female's eggs during spawning

mollusk an invertebrate with a smooth, soft body such as a clam or a snail

native an indigenous or naturally occurring species

omnivore a fish or animal that eats plants and animal matter

otolith an L-shaped bone found in the inner ear of fish

opercle bone covering the gills, also called gill cover or operculum

panfish small freshwater game fish that can be fried whole in a pan, such as crappies, perch and sunfish

pectoral fins paired fins on the side of the fish just behind the gills

pelagic fish species that live in open water, in the food-rich upper layer of water; not associated with the bottom

pelvic fins paired fins below or behind the pectoral fins on the bottom (ventral portion) of the fish

pharyngeal teeth tooth-like structures in the throat on the margins of the gill bars

pheromone a chemical scent secreted as a means of communication between members of the same species

piscivore a predatory fish that mainly eats other fish

planktivore a fish that feeds on plankton

plankton floating or weakly swimming aquatic plants and animals, including larval fish, that drift with the current; often eaten by fish; individual organisms are called plankters

plankton bloom a marked increase in the amount of plankton due to favorable conditions such as nutrients and light

range the geographic region in which a species is found

ray hard supporting part of the fin; resembles a spine but is jointed (can be raised and lowered) and is barbed; found in catfish, carp and goldfish

ray soft flexible structures supporting the fin membrane, sometimes branched

redd a nest-like depression made by a male or female fish during the spawn, often refers to nest of trout and salmon species

riparian area land adjacent to streams, rivers, lakes and other wetlands where the vegetation is influenced by the great availability of water

riprap rock or concrete used to protect a lake shore or river bank from erosion

roe fish eggs

scales small, flat plates covering the outer skin of many fish

Secchi disk a black-and-white circular disk used to measure water clarity; scientists record the average depth at which the disk disappears from sight when lowered into the water

silt small, easily disturbed bottom particles smaller than sand but larger than clay

siltation the accumulation of soil particles

spawning the process of fish reproduction; involves females laying eggs and males fertilizing them to produce young fish

spine stiff, pointed structures found along with soft rays in some fins; unlike hard rays they are not jointed

spiracle an opening on the posterior portion of the head above and behind the eye

standard length length of the fish from the mouth to the end of the vertebral column

stocking the purposeful, artificial introduction of a fish species into an area

substrate bottom composition of a lake, stream or river

subterminal mouth below the snout of the fish

swim bladder see air bladder

tailrace area immediately downstream of a dam or power plant

tapetum lucidum reflective pigment in a Walleye's eye

thermocline middle layer of water in a stratified lake, typically oxygen rich, characterized by a sharp drop in water temperature; often the lowest depth at which fish can be routinely found

terminal mouth forward facing

total length the length of the fish from the mouth to the tail compressed to its fullest length

tributary a stream that feeds into another stream, river or lake

turbid cloudy; water clouded by suspended sediments or plant matter that limits visibility and the passage of light

velocity the speed of water flowing in a stream or river

vent the opening at the end of the digestive tract

ventral the underside of the fish

vertebrate an animal with a backbone

vomerine teeth teeth on the roof of the mouth

warmwater a non-salmonid species of fish that lives in water that routinely exceeds 70 degrees; also used to describe a lake or river according to average summer temperature

yolk the part of an egg containing food for the developing fish

zooplankton the animal component of plankton; tiny animals that float or swim weakly; common food of fry and small fish

PRIMARY REFERENCES

Becker, G. C. 1983
Fishes of Wisconsin
University of Wisconsin Press

Eddy, S, Underhill, J. C. 1974
Northern Fishes
University of Minnesota Press

Hubbs, C. L. and Lagler, K. F. revised by Smith, G. R 2004
Fishes of the Great Lakes Region
University of Michigan Press

McClane, A. J. 1978
Freshwater Fishes of North America
Henry Holt and Company

Smith, P.W 1979
The Fish of Illinois
University of Illinois Press

Thomas, P. assisted by Callahan, E. 1993
Lake Erie Fish Illustrated
Allegheny Press Science Series No. 28

Trautman, M. B. 1957
The Fishes of Ohio
Ohio State University Press

INDEX

A

Alewife, 56
American Bream, see Golden Shiner
American Brook Lamprey, see
    Native Lamprey
American Eel, 46
American Roach, see Golden Shiner
Atlantic Eel, see: American Eel
Autumn Salmon, see: Pink Salmon

B

Baldpate, see: Bigmouth Buffalo
Baltimore Minnow, see Goldfish
Barfish, see Yellow Bass
Bass, Hybrid Striped, 184
Bass, Largemouth, 158
Bass, Rock, 180
Bass, Smallmouth, 160
Bass, Spotted, 162
Bass, Striped, 188
Bass, White, 186
Bay Fish, see: White Sucker
Bay Mullet, see Silver Redhorse
Bayou Bass, see: Largemouth Bass
Beaverfish, see: Bowfin
Big-eyed Herring, see: Alewife
Bighead Carp, 70
Bigheaded Sucker, see: Northern
    Hog Sucker
Bigmouth Buffalo, 142
Blackband Topminnow, see:
    Blackstripe Topminnow
Black Bass, see: Largemouth Bass
Black Buffalo, 144
Black Bullhead, 26
Black Crappie, 164

Blackhead Minnow, see: Fathead
    Minnow
Black Mouth, see: Chinook Salmon
Black Mullet, see: White Sucker
Black Redhorse, see Shorthead
    Redhorse
Blackspot Chub, see: Creek Chub
Blackstripe Topminnow, 192
Black Sturgeon, see: Lake Sturgeon
Blue-and-orange Sunfish, see:
    Longear Sunfish
Blueback, see: Coho Salmon
Blue Catfish, 32
Bluegill, 168
Blue Router, see: Bigmouth Buffalo
Blue Sunfish, see: Bluegill, Longear
    Sunfish
Boston Eel, see: American, Eel
Bowfin, 24
Brassy Bass, see Yellow Bass
Bream, see: Bluegill, Golden Shiner,
    Pumpkinseed
Broadnose Gar, see: Shortnose Gar
Bronzeback, see: Smallmouth Bass
Brook Chub, see: Creek Chub
Brookie, see: Brook Trout
Brook Silverside, 132
Brook Stickleback, 136
Brook Trout, 114
Brown Bullhead, 28
Brown Trout, 116
Bubbler, see: Freshwater Drum
Buffalo, Bigmouth, 142
Buffalo, Black, 144
Buffalo, Smallmouth, 146

200

Buglemouth, see: Common Carp
Bullhead, Black, 26
Bullhead, Brown, 28
Bullhead, Yellow, 30
Buoy Tender, see: Black Buffalo
Burbot, 42
Butterfish, see Golden Shiner

C

Carp, Bighead, 70
Carp, Common, 72
Carp, Grass, 74
Carp, Silver, 78
Carpsucker, see: Quillback
Catfish, Channel, 34
Catfish, Flathead, 36
Catfish, White, 38
Central Mudminnow, 92
Channel Catfish, 34
Chinook Salmon, 122
Chub, Creek, 80
Cisco, 128
Coarse-scaled Sucker, see: White
    Sucker
Coaster Trout, see: Brook Trout
Coho Salmon, 124
Common Bullhead, see: Black
    Bullhead
Common Carp, 72
Common Chub, see: Creek Chub
Common Cisco, see: Cisco
Common Eel, see: American Eel
Common Sculpin, see: Mottled
    Sculpin
Common Stickleback, see: Brook
    Stickleback
Common Sucker, see: White Sucker
Copperbelly, see: Bluegill

Crappie, Black, 164
Crappie, White, 166
Crawl-a-Bottom, see: Northern Hog
    Sucker
Creek Chub, 80
Croaker, see: Freshwater Drum
Current Buffalo, see: Black Buffalo
Cusk, see: Burbot
Cypress Trout, see: Bowfin

D

Dace, Southern Redbelly, 82
Darter, Johnny, 96
Deep-Water Buffalo, see: Black
    Buffalo
Dogfish, see: Bowfin, Central
    Mudminnow
Drum, Freshwater, 44
Duckbill, see: Paddlefish
Dwarf Sunfish, see: Orangespotted
    Sunfish

E

Eastern Sucker, see: White Sucker
Eel, American, 46
Eelpout, see: Burbot
Ellwife, see: Alewife
European Carp, see: Common Carp

F

Fathead Minnow, 84
Flathead Catfish, 36
Freshwater Drum, 44
Freshwater Eel, see: American Eel
Friar, see: Brook Silverside
Frost Fish, see: Rainbow Smelt

G

Garfish, see: Longnose Gar
Gar, Longnose, 48

German Brown, see: Brown Trout
German Carp, see: Common Carp
Gizzard Shad, 60
Goby, Round, 54
Goggle Eye, see: Rock Bass, Warmouth
Gold Bass, see: Yellow Bass
Golden Carp, see: Goldfish
Golden Redhorse, see: Shorthead Redhorse
Golden Shad, see: Alewife
Golden Shiner, 86
Goldeye, 88
Goldfish, 76
Grass Carp, 74
Grass Pickerel, 108
Grass Pike, see: Grass Pickerel
Greater Redhorse, see Shorthead Redhorse
Great Gray Trout, see: Lake Trout
Great Lakes Cisco, see: Cisco
Great Lakes Longear, see: Longear Sunfish
Great Lakes Muskellunge, see: Muskellunge
Great Northern Pickerel, see: Northern Pike
Green Bass, see: Largemouth Bass
Green Perch, see: Green Sunfish
Green Sunfish, 170
Green Trout, see: Largemouth Bass
Grinder, see: Freshwater Drum
Grindle, see: Bowfin
Gudgeon, see: Mottled Sculpin

H

Hackleback, see: Shovelnose Sturgeon
Hammerhandle, see: Northern Pike

Hammerhead, see: Northern Hog Sucker
Herring, Skipjack, 58
Hickory Shad, see: Gizzard Shad
Highback Buffalo, see: Smallmouth Buffalo
Hog Molly, see: Northern Hog Sucker
Hog Sucker, Northern, 154
Horned Dace, see: Creek Chub
Horned Pout, see: Black Bullhead
Humpback Buffalo, see Smallmouth Buffalo
Humpback Salmon, see: Pink Salmon
Humpy, see: Pink Salmon
Hybrid Striped Bass, 184

I

Ice Fish, see: Rainbow Smelt
Indiana Minnow, see Goldfish

J

Jack, see: Northern Pike; Walleye
Jackfish, see: Northern Pike; Sauger; Walleye
Jack Perch, see: Yellow Perch
Jack Salmon, see: Sauger
Jack Shad, see: Gizzard Shad
Johnny Darter, 96

K

Kamloops Trout, see: Rainbow Trout
Kentucky Bass, see: Spotted Bass
King Salmon, see: Chinook Salmon

L

Lake Bass, see: White Bass
Lake Fish, see: Bighead Carp
Lake Herring, see: Cisco, Rainbow Smelt
Lake Lamprey, see: Sea Lamprey

Lake Lawyer, see: Bowfin
Lake Quillback, see: Quillback
Laker, see: Lake Trout
Lake Sturgeon, 138
Lake Trout, 118
Lamprey, Sea, 66
Lampreys, Native, 64
Landlocked Lamprey, see: Sea
    Lamprey
Largemouth Bass, 158
Lawyer, see: Burbot
Least Brook Lamprey, see: Native
    Lampreys
Leatherback, see: Southern
    Redbelly Dace
Leather Carp, see: Common Carp
Leefish, see: Rainbow Smelt
Ling, see: Burbot
Little Pickerel, see: Grass Pickerel
Loch Leven Trout, see: Brown Trout
Log Darter, see Logperch
Logperch, 104
Longear Sunfish, 172
Longnose Gar, 48
Longtail Sucker, see Silver Redhorse

M

Mackinaw, see: Lake Trout
Madtom, Tadpole, 40
Manitou Darter, see Logperch
Many-spined Stickleback, see:
    Brook Stickleback
Marbled Bullhead, see: Brown
    Bullhead
Marble-eyes, see: Walleye
Minnow, Fathead, 84
Mirror Carp, see: Common Carp

Mississippi Cat, see: Blue Catfish,
    Flathead Catfish
Mississippi Mudminnow, see:
    Central Mudminnow
Missouri Minnow, see Goldfish
Mongrel, see: Bigmouth Buffalo
Mooneye, 90
Mosquitofish, 68
Mosquito Minnow, see
    Mosquitofish
Mottled Sculpin, 130
Mountain Trout, see: Smallmouth
    Bass
Mud Cat, see: Flathead Catfish
Mud Chub, see: Creek Chub
Muddler, see: Mottled Sculpin
Mudfish, see: Bowfin; Central
    Mudminnow
Mudminnow, Central, 92
Mud Pickerel, see: Grass Pickerel
Mud Pike, see: Grass Pickerel
Mud Shad, see: Gizzard Shad
Muskellunge, 110
Muskie, see: Muskellunge

N

Native Lampreys, 64
Northern Brook Lamprey, see:
    Native Lampreys
Northern Hog Sucker, 154
Northern Horned Dace, see: Creek
    Chub
Longear Sunfish, 172
Northern Pike, 112
Northern Redhorse, see Shorthead
    Redhorse
Northern Silverside, see: Brook
    Silverside

O

Ohio Lamprey, see: Native Lampreys
Ohio Muskellunge, see: Muskellunge
Orangespot, see: Orangespotted Sunfish
Orangespotted Sunfish, 174

P

Pacific Trout, see: Rainbow Trout
Paddlefish, 94
Pale Crappie, see: White Crappie
Papermouth, see: Black Crappie; White Crappie
Pickerel, Grass, 108
Pied Cat, see: Flathead Catfish
Pike, Northern, 112
Pink Salmon, 126
Pond Shiner, see Golden Shiner
Prairie Buffalo, see: Bigmouth Buffalo
Pumpkinseed, 176
Punky, see: Pumpkinseed
Pygmy Sunfish, see: Orangespotted Sunfish

Q

Quillback, 148
Quinnat, see: Chinook Salmon

R

Rainbow Smelt, 134
Rainbow Trout, 120
Razorback Buffalo, see Smallmouth Buffalo
Redbelly Dace, see: Southern Redbelly Dace
Red Cat, see: Brown Bullhead
Redear Sunfish, 178
Redeye, see: Rock Bass, Smallmouth Bass

Redeye Bass, see: Smallmouth Bass
Redfin Mullet, see Silver Redhorse
Redhorse, Shorthead, 150
Redhorse, Silver, 152
Red Perch, see: Longear Sunfish
Red-Sided Darter, see: Johnny Darter
Red Sturgeon, see: Lake Sturgeon
Riffle Sucker, see: Northern Hog Sucker
Ringed Crappie, see: White Crappie
Ringed Perch, see: Yellow Perch
River Carp, see: Bighead Carp
River Cat, see Blue Catfish
Rivereye, see: Saugeye
River Herring, see: Alewife, Skipjack Herring
River Pike, see: Sauger
River Redhorse, see Shorthead Redhorse
River Whitefish, see: Mooneye
Roach, see Golden Shiner
Rock Bass, 180
Rockfish, see: Striped Bass
Rock Sturgeon, see: Lake Sturgeon
Rock Sunfish, see: Rock Bass
Round Buffalo, see: Bigmouth Buffalo, Black Buffalo
Round Goby, 54
Round Sunfish, see: Pumpkinseed
Router, see: Bigmouth Buffalo

S

Salmon, Chinook, 122
Salmon, Coho, 124
Salmon, Pink, 126
Sand Bass, see: Green Sunfish; White Bass
Sand Minnow, see: Trout-perch

Sand Pike, see: Sauger
Sand Sturgeon, see: Shovelnose
    Sturgeon
Sauger, 98
Saugeye, 100
Saugie, see: Saugeye
Sawbelly, see: Alewife
Sculpin, Mottled, 130
Sea Lamprey, 66
Sea Perch, see: White Perch
Sea Trout, see: Coho Salmon
Shad, Gizzard, 60
Shallow Water Cisco, see: Cisco
Sheepshead, see: Freshwater Drum
Shellcracker, see: Redear Sunfish
Shiner Carp, see: Silver Carp
Ship Goby, see: Round Goby
Shortbilled Gar, see Shortnose Gar
Shorthead Redhorse, 150
Shortnose Gar, 50
Shovelhead, see: Flathead Catfish
Shovelnose, see: Flathead Catfish
Shovelnose Sturgeon, 140
Silver Bass, see: White Bass
Silver Carp, 78; see also: Quillback
Silver Cat, see Blue Catfish
Silver Catfish, see: Channel, White
    Catfish
Silver Chub, see: Creek Chub
Silver Crappie, see: White Crappie
Silver Lamprey, see: Native Lampreys
Silver Mullet, see Silver Redhorse
Silver Redhorse, 152
Silver Salmon, see: Coho Salmon
Silver Shad, see Threadfin Shad
Silverside, Brook, 132
Silver Trout, see: Rainbow Trout

Skipjack, see: Brook Silverside
Skipjack Herring, 58
Skipper, see Skipjack Herring
Slicker, see: Mooneye
Slough Bass, see: Largemouth Bass
Smallheaded Mullet, see: Golden
    Redhorse
Smallmouth Bass, 160
Smallmouth Buffalo, 146
Smelt, Rainbow, 134
Smoothback Sturgeon, see: Lake
    Sturgeon
Snot Rocket, see: Northern Pike
Southern Redbelly Dace, 82
Speck, see: Black Crappie
Speckled Amur, see: Bighead Carp
Speckled Bass, see: Spotted Bass
Speckled Bullhead, see: Brown
    Bullhead
Speckled Catfish, see: Channel
    Catfish
Speckled Gar, see Spotted Gar
Speckled Perch, see: Black Crappie
Speckled Trout, see: Brook Trout
Spiny Minnow, see: Brook Stickleback
Splake, 118
Spoonbill Cat, see: Paddlefish
Spot, see Spotted Bass
Spotfin Pike, see: Sauger
Spotted Bass, 162
Spotted Catfish, see: Channel Catfish
Spotted Gar, 53
Spotted Trout, see: Brown Trout
Spring Salmon, see: Chinook Salmon
Squaretail Trout, see: Brook Trout
Steelhead, see: Rainbow Trout
Stickleback, Brook, 136

Stonecat, 40
Stone Sturgeon, see: Lake Sturgeon
Strawberry Bass, see: Bluegill
Streaker, see: Striped Bass; White Bass
Striped Bass, 188
Striped Bass, Hybrid, 184
Striped Perch, see: Yellow Perch
Striper, see: Striped Bass
Stubnose Gar, see Shortnose Gar
Stumpknocker, see: Redear Sunfish;
    Warmouth
Sturgeon, Lake, 138
Sturgeon, Shovelnose, 140
Sucker, Northern Hog, 154
Sucker, White, 156
Sun Bass, see: Pumpkinseed
Sunfish, Green, 170
Sunfish, Longear, 172
Sunfish, Orangespotted, 174
Sunfish, Redear, 178
Sun Perch, see: Bluegill
Surface Minnow, see Mosquitofish
Surf Bass, see: Striped Bass
Susquehanna Salmon, see: Walleye
Switchtail, see: Shovelnose Sturgeon

T

Tadpole Madtom, 40
Tank Goby, see: Round Goby
Thick-lipped Buffalo, see
    Smallmouth Buffalo
Threadfin Shad, 62
Thread Shad, see Threadfin Shad
Thunderpumper, see: Freshwater
    Drum
Tiger Muskie, see: Muskellunge
Togue, see: Lake Trout
Toothed Herring, see: Goldeye,

Mooneye
Topminnow, Blackstripe, 192
Trout, Brook, 114
Trout, Brown, 116
Trout, Lake, 118
Trout, Rainbow, 120
Tuffy, see: Fathead Minnow
Tullibee, see: Cisco
Tyee, see: Chinook Salmon

W

Walleye, 102
Walleyed Pike, see: Walleye
Warmouth, 182
Weed Bass, see Warmouth
Weed Catfish, see: White Catfish
Weed Darter, see: Johnny Darter
Western Goldeye, see: Goldeye
Western Mudminnow, see: Central
    Mudminnow
White Amur, see: Grass Carp
White Bass, 186
White Cat, see Blue Catfish
White Catfish, 38
White Crappie, 166
White Perch, see: Freshwater Drum
Whitenose Redhorse, see Silver
    Redhorse
White Shad, see: Mooneye
White Striper, see: Hybrid Striped
    Bass
White Sucker, 156
White Trout, see: Smallmouth Bass
White-whiskered Bullhead, see:
    Yellow Bullhead
Whitey, see: White Catfish
Widemouth Sunfish, see Warmouth
Willow Cat, see: Stonecat

206

Winnipeg Goldeye, see: Goldeye
Wiper, see: Hybrid Striped Bass

Y

Yellow Bass, 190
Yellowbelly Dace, see: Southern
    Redbelly Dace
Yellowbelly Darter, see: Johnny
    Darter
Yellow Bream, see: Redear Sunfish
Yellow Bullhead, 30
Yellow Cat, see: Flathead Catfish,
    Yellow Bullhead
Yellow Herring, see: Goldeye
Yellow Perch, 106
Yellow Shad, see Threadfin Shad
Yellow Sunfish, see: Pumpkinseed

Z

Zebrafish, see Logperch

ABOUT THE AUTHOR

Dave Bosanko was born in Kansas and studied engineering before following his love of nature to degrees in biology and chemistry from Emporia State University. He spent thirty years as staff biologist at two of the University of Minnesota's field stations. Though his training was in mammal physiology, Dave worked on a wide range of research projects ranging from fish, bird and mammal population studies to experiments with biodiversity and prairie restoration. A lifelong fisherman and avid naturist, he is now spending his retirement writing, fishing and traveling.